AF616499

KOHELETH | ספר קהלת

Life and its Meaning

ספר קהלת

KOHELETH

Life and its Meaning

עם

פירוש רש״י

ערוך מחדש בידי יוסף שמואל פוגל

A modern translation and interpretation
of the Book of Ecclesiastes / *by*

HAROLD I. LEIMAN

Jerusalem / New York FELDHEIM PUBLISHERS

עריכת פירוש רש"י שבמהדורה זו
נעשתה מתוך השוואה מדוייקת בין מהדורות שונות
ובבירור מקורות בדברי חז"ל

התעתיק והתרגום לאנגלית
של הלועזים בפירוש רש"י
נעשו לפי הספר

The transliteration and translation of the *lo'azim* (words in Old French) in the commentary of Rashi are based on
Arsène Darmesteter, *Les gloses françaises de Raschi dans la Bible,* Paris 1909

כל הזכויות בטקסט העברי
ובפירוש רש"י במהדורה זו
שמורות למוציאים לאור
© 1978
הוצאת ספרים פלדהיים בע"מ
ירושלים

ISBN 0-87306-143-8
Published 1978

Translation and Commentary
Copyright © 1978 by
Harold I. Leiman

All rights reserved. No part of this publication may be reproduced, stored in a retrieval system or transmitted, in any form or by any means, electronic, mechanical, photocopying, recording or otherwise, without the prior permission of the copyright owner.

FELDHEIM PUBLISHERS
POB 35002 / Jerusalem, Israel

200 Airport Executive Park
Spring Valley, NY 10977

Printed in Israel

Dedicated

to the memory of

Shraga Feivel Mendlowitz

זצ״ל

"...*one upright man in a thousand*" (7:28)

CONTENTS

PREFACE

ינחני במעגלי צדק למען שמו

Professor Joseph Babor excelled as a teacher of chemistry; he was inspired and his lectures were inspiring. Painstaking efforts helped to make the lesson an exciting adventure; fascinating demonstrations illustrated each lecture. He collected ideas from colleagues and materials from all sources, even from books on magic. And yet the professor was never satisfied; he always sought newer and better approaches.

One day he chanced into the bookstore of an old acquaintance. After some friendly chatter, the professor asked as if by compulsion, "Would you get me a good textbook on classroom demonstrations in chemistry?"

"If you'll write it yourself," said the bookdealer, "I'll be glad to furnish you a copy."

From my early youth I sought to understand some of the difficult and seemingly heretical passages of Koheleth. Over the years I followed the comments of our Sages and the traditional commentators as well as recent commentaries in several languages. Unfortunately, many of these later writers and translators, who sought to adhere closely to the literal meaning, did so at the expense of the sacredness of the text. In vain did I plead with scholarly friends to write a modern commentary that would befit the Solomonic authorship.

I remarked to my wife, Harriet, that I was disappointed

that no one had written the commentary I sought; that I felt was much needed.

"If you'll write it yourself," she said, "I'll be glad to do the typing."

It was an offer I could not refuse; I accepted the challenge. This is the end-product. No doubt it is insignificant in proportion to the amount of time and effort I have devoted to its preparation. I know, too, that I have hardly scratched the surface in this attempt to fathom the depth of the wisdom of Solomon. However, if this commentary will help some individual to find Koheleth somewhat smoother reading, if it will help another to see a glimmer of light toward the resolution of one of the basic life problems touched upon by Koheleth, I will have been amply rewarded.

"There is nothing new under the sun," said Koheleth. Certainly there can be very little originality in a commentary on part of the Bible. Indirectly, of course, I have learnt from all those who preceded me. Because I have stood on the shoulders of our Sages and the commentators who followed them, I was able to see a small albeit winding clearance through that forest called Koheleth. My wife provided constructive suggestions besides doing tiresome typing through many revisions. My sons, Y'hoshua and Shnayer Zalman, reviewed the manuscript and made very significant critical comments. I am greatly indebted to them for their help. Responsibility for error or misinterpretation, however, is strictly my own.

I am especially thankful to my publisher, Mr. Yaakov Feldheim, who graciously consented to include a well-documented text of Rashi despite the considerable expense involved. Rabbi Elchanan Wengrov, editor for Feldheim Publishers, has provided invaluable assistance throughout the entire publication process. It is due to his merit and unusual talents that the book has emerged in its present attractive form.

Rashi is the father of all commentators. In Rashi one finds basic concepts culled from חז"ל; in Rashi one is guided to the deeper meaning alluded to by the text. It is therefore a distinct advantage to have the Rashi immediately available. Those who are able to study the text and Rashi in the original will find the experience rewarding and enriching over and above anything that a later commentator could provide. Most important, they will find that there is still much to be learnt from Koheleth in the areas of פרד"ס.

Shraga Feivel Mendlowitz, to whom this work is dedicated, has done more for Torah education in the United States than any other single individual. His love for Torah was equalled only by his love for Eretz Yisrael; his modesty was matched only by his selflessness. In word and deed he was a teacher par excellence. The spirit of the *tanach* flowed through his arteries and veins. When I think — to mention only one instance — of the time he taught us "By the waters of Babylon, there we sat down and wept, when we remembered Zion," I can still feel myself drawn into the vortex of the experience.

Were he alive today and were I to place this work before him, he would have smiled broadly. Nothing made him happier than achievement, even the minutest achievement, on the part of his pupils. But he would have taken out that confounded pocket watch, shown it to me and said, "You're late again."

H. I. Leiman

ירושלים, עיה"ק
Jerusalem
3 Elul 5736

INTRODUCTION

The Book of Ecclesiastes (Koheleth) has been a relatively closed book to the average reader of the Bible for more than two millennia. It presents difficulties from many aspects, including structure, organization and content. An arbitrary division of chapters sometimes separates two verses that should be logically united. Many varied and disconnected thoughts appear abruptly in any one chapter; the language is sometimes difficult and elusive. A pessimistic prologue, followed at times by apparently pessimistic statements, gives the impression that the book proposes a life of abstinence, when in truth its message is happiness and its attainment. Heterodoxical as well as contradictory statements only serve to puzzle the reader and make him wonder how the book was ever admitted to the canon.

The older commentators, who had faith in the integrity and objective honesty of the Talmudic sages, accepted the traditional text and the Solomonic authorship. Whenever the text was heterodox or contradictory, they offered a hermeneutical interpretation of the whole verse. These interpretations clarified concepts, but it was frequently difficult to see how the thought fitted into the verse.

Modern commentators generally took a more brazen and irreverent way out of the difficulties; they approached the

Book of Koheleth with an anatomist's scalpel. Certain verses were assigned to interpolative editors, others were simply discarded. After the surgery was performed a body of verses remained which seemed more consistent. This they assigned to some unknown "wisdom" writer. They considered this procedure to be justified because the language and thought of the Book of Koheleth did not, in the opinion of these commentators, reflect the thinking of the Solomonic age. Therefore, a more "scientifically" acceptable Book of Koheleth was needed. One is amazed that the conclusions of the Talmudic sages, who lived so much closer in time to the author, are so callously dismissed. After all, the Rabbis, who were respected for their scrupulous honesty and disciplined scholarship, were not likely to finally admit to the canon and accept as Solomonic a work whose authorship was dubious with respect to language, thought or any other criterion.

The present writer accepts the traditional text and Solomonic authorship as reflected in that text itself. The writer finds the content of Koheleth consistent with Solomon's thoughts in Proverbs and with David's thinking in the Psalms. In fact, only a careful study of the Psalms and Proverbs will throw light on some of the abstruse passages in the Book of Koheleth. A fragmented study of Koheleth creates more problems than solutions. However, when Koheleth is viewed as a description of the inner struggle in man — of the battle between reason and emotion, between the spiritual and the material, between optimism and pessimism — then the heterodoxy and contradictions are ameliorated and frequently resolved.

Koheleth (Solomon) was a diligent teacher. Like every good teacher he started at the level of understanding of his pupils. He would win them over by repeating their statements, no matter how heretical, in all seriousness. Then he would hold the statements up to the light and examine them. Frequently he would sprinkle his talk with skeptical thoughts that had been part of his own inner struggle. These, no doubt, delighted his listeners; they felt that he was one of them. And, indeed, he *was* one of them. In spite of his royal blood, he understood the problems and inner strife of the intelligent and faithful among the common folk. However, right from the start he informed them that everything emanated from Elohim (God) and that he did not waver in his faith for one moment. Forty times he mentions Elohim in this rather brief book, and he concludes the book with the statement that unless man fears Elohim he cannot attain the higher virtues which alone bring happiness.

Some of the basic problems that have troubled philosophers from time immemorial are tackled by Koheleth. What is happiness? How does one attain happiness? Why is there evil? Why do some righteous people suffer and some wicked ones prosper? Is man free to do as he pleases or are all his actions determined?

These problems are of such universal interest that it is a pity that Ecclesiastes (Koheleth) has not been more readily accessible to the readers of the Bible. The present work is an attempt by the writer to make the text more readable and understandable through a modern translation and commentary. Especially in the present day, when there is so much moral confusion, when so many are searching for meaning in life, Koheleth has a major contribution to make. It is a book for all time because it deals with the problems of all time.

About the Author

Koheleth (Solomon) was of royal blood; he was strongly influenced by his father, King David, author of the Psalms.

Unlike his father, he was able to relax and enjoy life; his reign was a peaceful and prosperous one (I Kings 5:5).

He became world-famous for his wisdom. His major occupation was the study of man and the world of nature. All the universe was his text.

> And he spoke of trees, from the cedar that
> is in Lebanon to the hyssop that springs
> out of the wall; he spoke also of beasts,
> and of fowl, and of creeping things, and
> of fishes. (I Kings 5:13)

Living itself was a thrilling experience for him. He enjoyed the beautiful in nature, in art, in music, and in women. He acquired for himself worldly enjoyments and participated in spiritual pursuits (Koheleth 2:3–10). He created thousands of proverbs and songs (I Kings 5:12). His three major works, accepted in the canon, are Proverbs, Song of Songs and Koheleth. The last might be described as his book of evaluation, wherein he evaluates various styles of living and offers guidance for those who seek the good life.

Koheleth (Solomon) was a happy man; he found delight in study and in his natural surroundings. It is a mistake to assume, because of the pessimistic passages in the Book of Koheleth, that he led a life of misery. Actually, these passages deplore modes of living which lead to unhappiness. And on the positive side, Koheleth urges man to eat, live and be merry. Seven times, in this work, he reminds us that God wants man to enjoy life. Solomon was wise, worldly and happy and in the Book of Koheleth he tells us, from personal experience and after mature contemplation, what to avoid in order that we, too, might achieve happiness.

Though he was raised in a kingly household, Koheleth showed no aloofness. He was a man of the people. Indeed, we find numerous instances in the Book of Koheleth where the author deplores oppression and the failure to respect human dignity. This characteristic he developed, no doubt, under the influence of his father, David, who in dedicating a Psalm to Solomon, pleaded:

> May he judge the poor of the people,
> And save the children of the needy,
> and crush the oppressor. (Psalms 72:4)

Koheleth loved his people and loved all mankind. At the dedication of the First Temple, which he built, a considerable portion of his prayer was a plea to God to forgive the repentant whether they be the entire people or whether it be an individual (I Kings 8:35–36). This is followed by a supplication to God to accept the prayer of all mankind as well:

> Moreover, concerning the stranger
> That is not of Your people Israel,
> When he shall come out of a far country
> For Your name's sake —
> For they shall hear of Your great name,
> And of Your mighty hand
> When he shall come and pray toward this house;
> May You hear in Your dwelling-place, heaven,
> And do all that the stranger
> Calls to You for. (I Kings 8:41–43)

The author of Koheleth, then, studied man and respected man, and we shall expect to find this high regard for man reflected in the Book of Koheleth. Nor should we be surprised to find that Koheleth criticizes severely any attempt by man to belittle or to usurp the rights of his fellow man.

Philosophy of Koheleth

Koheleth (Solomon) was conversant with so many subjects that it would make a lengthy volume in itself to fully discuss all of these as expressed in his writings. However, there are three major themes in the Book of Koheleth which serve as pillars of the author's philosophy. These are: Elohim, good and evil, and man. What follows is mainly the background for these themes as found in Solomon's other works, as well as in the Psalms of David.

A / ELOHIM

Many forms exist for the expression of the Divinity in the Hebrew language and tradition. In his Koheleth, Solomon has chosen to use the term "Elohim" exclusively. He did so perhaps because that is the aspect of the Divinity most easily comprehended by the average man. Elohim is the name used to depict God as the Creator:

> In the beginning, Elohim created heaven and earth.
> (Genesis 1:1)

Koheleth also expects his community to recognize Elohim as Providence (2:24). Not only did Elohim create the world, but He continually provides His creatures with their needs and controls all that takes place in the world.

Elohim as judge is another aspect reflected in the Book of Koheleth. The Hebrew tradition associates the name Elohim with justice in contradistinction to the Tetragrammaton, which is associated with mercy. In Exodus 22:8, the word *elohim* is used to mean judge. Koheleth says (11:9), "Follow the dictates of your heart and the desires of your eyes, but know that Elohim will bring you to *judgment* for all these things."

In the Psalms, David depicts yet another nuance of Elohim. He, too, distinguishes between Elohim and the Tetragrammaton. According to David, the former represents the appearance of the Lord as He manifests Himself in the creation; the latter represents the essence of the Lord. But man, whose mind is finite, cannot grasp the essence of the Lord, who is infinite. Therefore, man's appreciation of the Lord is confined to His appearance in the creation — the Elohim of creation.

Just as man cannot stare into the sun without using a shield for his eyes, so can he not form a concept of the essence of the Lord except through His appearances in the universe as Elohim.

> As the sun and a shield so the
> Tetragrammaton and Elohim. (Psalms 84:12)

Solomon, like his father, David, saw the lack of the fear of Elohim as the source of man's wickedness. Man-made laws never were adequate to build a just society, free of oppression. The family tradition has it that depravity, corruption and oppression are characteristic of a godless society:

> The withered man has said in his heart
> There is no Elohim;
> They have dealt corruptly, and have done
> abominable inquity;
> There is none that do good.
> Elohim looked down from heaven upon the children
> of men,
> To see whether there was any man of understanding
> who was searching for Elohim.
> Every one of them became unclean;
> All together they became impure.
> None was a doer of good,
> None, not even one of them. (Psalms 53:2–4)

Sometimes the wicked man is pictured as the slave of his desires and passions, sometimes as the proud and rational individual who seeks out philosophies and theories to deny the existence of Elohim. The following passage describes the latter:

> The wicked man, in the pride of his countenance,
> Cares for naught.
> "There is no Elohim!" —
> That is the essence of all his plans. (Psalms 10:4)

As the inheritor of this tradition, there is little wonder that Koheleth sees, in the fear of Elohim, all of man. Man, even the average man, is able to perceive the presence of Elohim in the universe. Man has freedom of choice to do or not to do his duty by God and man. The fear of Elohim should enable him to pursue the path of the righteous, to serve God and to respect his fellow-man.

B / GOOD AND EVIL

The many instances of evil and vanity cited by Koheleth would seem to indicate that the problem of evil was uppermost in the minds of his audience. Why should there be evil? Why should there be wicked who prosper? Why should there be righteous who suffer? These are some of the grievances implicit and explicit throughout the Book of Koheleth.

The roots of the complaint are already found in the Psalms, where David asks:

> Why, O Lord, do you stand far off
> And hide Your presence in times of trouble?
> Through the pride of the wicked
> The poor is pursued.
> They are caught in the plots
> That they have conceived. (Psalms 10:1–2)

The Psalmist admits that even he at one time was envious of the wicked:

For I was envious of the arrogant,
When I saw the prosperity of the wicked.
For there are no pangs at their death,
And their body is sound.
In the trouble of man they are not;
Neither are they plagued like man. (Psalms 73:3–5)

David offers no explanation for the oppression of the poor by the arrogant or for the prosperity of the wicked. But he does argue that evil in the form of punishment is meant for man's ultimate good. Man should look upon suffering as an atonement for some iniquity or as a warning to improve:

You have chastised man for iniquity...
(Psalms 39:12)

If man can accept justice and discipline as gracefully as he accepts the good things in life, then there is no absolute evil. Whether the Lord has dealt with him in loving-kindness or whether He has punished him in judgment, man should still express gratitude:

A Psalm of David:
I will sing of loving-kindness and of justice,
To You, O Lord, will I address my song.
(Psalms 101:1)
Happy is the man whom You chastise, O Lord...
(Psalms 94:12)

Koheleth (Solomon) accepts the above premise and compares the situation to the wholesome relationship between a loving father and an understanding son:

Whom the Lord loves He chastises,
Even as a father the son in whom he delights.
(Proverbs 3:12)

Despite the many faces of evil, Solomon holds that the good in the universe outweighs the evil by far. This very positive approach is inherited from his father, David, author of the Psalms — all of which are songs. Both his troubles and his joys are expressed by David in song — an approach possible only when one views even evil as an instrument for man's ultimate good.

Creation and natural phenomena serve as sources of inspiration for David and Solomon. Even the simplest things, life itself, light, and sunshine, are subjects worthy of study and contemplation. They call forth a profound sense of gratitude and praise:

> The heavens recount the glory of God
> And the firmament tells the work of His Hands.
> (Psalms 19:2)

> The young lions roar after their prey
> And to seek their food from God.
> When the sun rises they steal away
> And crouch in their dens.
> Then man goes forth to his work,
> And to his employment until evening.
> How manifold are Your works, O Lord;
> You made them all in wisdom;
> The earth is full of Your creatures.
> (Psalms 104:21–24)

> The flowers appear on the earth;
> The time of singing is come,
> And the voice of the turtle-dove is heard in our land.
> (Song of Songs 2:12)

C / MAN

Koheleth (Solomon) is very discriminating about his choice of the ideal man. He states that he has found only one in a thousand. What are some of the characteristics of this very rare man?

David seeks moral integrity, social justice, respect for human dignity and the love of truth:

A Psalm of David:
O Lord, who will live in Your tent?
Who will dwell on Your holy mountain?
He who walks in moral integrity, and practices
righteousness
And speaks the truth in his heart,
He who has borne no slander on his tongue,
Nor done evil to his fellow,
Nor tolerated an aspersion cast upon his neighbor.
(Psalms 15:1–3)

Later on David mentions wisdom as characteristic of the righteous:

The mouth of the righteous utters wisdom . . .
(Psalms 37:30)

Solomon places great emphasis upon wisdom:

The beginning of wisdom is: Get wisdom,
And in all your getting, get understanding.
(Proverbs 4:7)
Happy is the man who finds wisdom . . .
(Proverbs 3:13)

The ideal man fears the Lord, enjoys his work and is happy with what he possesses:

Happy is every one who fears the Lord,
Who walks in His ways.
When you eat the labor of your hands
You will be happy, and it will be well with you.
(Psalms 128:1–2)

In the Psalms, David states that the ideal man recognizes that it is not his might or his wisdom that earns him wealth, but rather the considerable assistance and blessing granted him by the Lord:

> If the Lord does not build a house,
> Then its builders have labored in vain upon it:
> If the Lord will not guard a city,
> The watchman has watched in vain. (Psalms 127:1)

The man who places his faith in the Lord need not labor incessantly, for the Lord can provide his needs even if he expends less effort:

> It is vain for you that you rise early
> And sit up late,
> You that eat the bread of toil;
> So He gives His loved ones even in sleep.
> (Psalms 127:2)

The ideal man is blessed with happy family life:

> Behold, children are an inheritance of the Lord:
> The fruit of the womb is a reward. (Psalms 127:3)

The man of Koheleth is in control of his emotions and thinks logically:

> He that is slow to anger is of great understanding,
> But he that is hasty of spirit exalts folly.
> (Proverbs 14:29)

The ideal man lives among his people and cooperates with them, lending a helping hand whenever he is able to:

> Do not withhold good from him to whom it is due,
> When it is in the power of your hand to do it.
> (Proverbs 3:27)

Perhaps the most terse description that fits the one man in a thousand is the condensed version supplied in another Psalm by David:

> He who has clean hands and a pure heart,
> Who has not lifted up his soul, which is Mine, unto vanity,
> And has not sworn deceitfully. (Psalms 24:4)

Happiness

The Book of Koheleth was written to guide man in the attainment of happiness. Throughout the book, Solomon reminds us that man's only function is to live the happy life. All along we have the feeling that the author is removing the obstacles that block our vision of the road to happiness. Soon we are to reach that most elusive highway. But somehow we never get there. Why doesn't Koheleth provide us with a list of specific items that will guarantee the happy life?

Koheleth is very clear about the modes of living which lead to unhappiness. He deplores them and illustrates the pathetic plight of those who pursue such courses. He describes experiments that he performed in order to achieve happiness — experiments that proved to be unsuccessful. Why is Koheleth not equally clear about what brings happiness in its wake?

Perhaps this is because there is no cut-and-dried recipe for happiness. Koheleth wisely provides only guidelines. It is for the reader to use these guidelines in developing his personal philosophy of life — a philosophy adapted to his condition and his peculiar circumstances. There is no specific formula that applies to every individual in every environment. Koheleth believes that he performs the greatest service to man by telling us what to avoid. This is more than half the battle. The rest of the philosophy of happiness is for each of us to develop — each according to his particular situation. Koheleth opens doors for us by suggesting many approaches to the good life. It is for us to enter some or all of these doors and fashion for ourselves a way of living which will guide us to happiness in our individual lives.

Chapter 1

ELOHIM

As the hart pants for the springs of water,
so my soul thirsts for you, Elohim.

Psalms

א] דִּבְרֵי קֹהֶלֶת בֶּן־דָּוִד מֶלֶךְ בִּירוּשָׁלִָם:

(א) **דברי קהלת.** כל מקום שנאמר דברי אינו אלא דברי תוכחות: (דברים א:א) אלה הדברים אשר דבר משה — (שם לב:טו) וישמן ישרון; (עמוס א:א) דברי עמוס — (שם ד:א) שמעו (את) הדבר הזה פרות הבשן; (ירמיה א:א) דברי ירמיהו — (שם ל:ו) שאלו־נא וראו אם־ילד זכר וגו׳; (שמואל ב׳, כג:א) ואלה דברי דוד — (שם כג:ו) ובליעל כקוץ מנד כלהם; דברי קהלת — וזרח השמש [וגו׳] כל הנחלים הולכים אל הים, כינה את הרשעים בחמה ולבנה וים שאין להם מתנת שכר — כך שנוי בספרי (דברים א), ולמדתי משם שהענין מדבר ברשעים, והמשילם לתגבורת החמה שסופה שוקעת. תוספת, דבר אחר: כל הנחלים הולכים אל הים, מה תלמוד לומר? בעובדי עבודה זרה נאמר שוטים המשתחוים למים, סבורים שיש בהם ממש לפי שרואין את הים הגדול, שכל הנחלים הולכים בו והוא אינו מלא, ואינן יודעין להבין כי אל המקום שהנחלים הולכים, שם הם שבים ללכת, שמימי הנהרות ההולכים לתוך הים הם המים עצמם שהלכו כבר; הם נובעים מתחת התהום והולכים למעלה מן הקרקע עד הים וחוזרים ונובעים, לפיכך אין הנהרות פוסקים ואין הים מלא ולא מפני שיש בהן ממש, עד כאן: **קהלת.** על שם שקיהל חכמות הרבה, וכן במקום אחר קוראו (משלי ל:א) אגור בן (יקא) [יקה], שאגר כל החכמה והקיאה (תנחומא וארא ה); ויש אומרים, שהיה אומר כל דבריו בהקהל (ע׳ קהלת רבה): **מלך בירושלם.** עיר החכמה:

1–11 / Prologue

1] Koheleth. The oldest and most reliable source for the authorship of Koheleth is the book itself, which has been admitted to the canon. Verses 1:1 and 1:12 provide details about the author. The only one who answers the description is Solomon. Then why does he call himself Koheleth and why has he named the book Koheleth? The Rabbis state that the name Koheleth derives from the word *kahal,* which means group or assembly. Solomon taught *kahal* after *kahal,* group after group, and tried to reach all the people. He weighed and probed and even fashioned many proverbs to make his thoughts more palatable to the people. Toward the close of

1] The words of Koheleth, son of David, king in
Jerusalem.

the book, in verse 12:9, it is stated explicitly, "And besides that Koheleth was wise, he also taught the people knowledge, weighing and probing and fashioning many proverbs."

We may reasonably assume that the words of heterodoxy found in the book of Koheleth are really the words of *kahal* that are reflected in some of the outpourings of Koheleth. The reverent and frequent use of Elohim (God) by Koheleth leaves no doubt as to the firmness of his belief. Thus the various heterodoxical teachings cannot be attributed in the first instance to Koheleth. In fact, it appears that the aim of Koheleth in this book is to subtly establish the kingdom of Elohim in the universe.

He gives the fullest expression to the blasphemy of the *kahal*; he describes experiments with hedonism; he describes graphically the inequities and evils faced by mankind. All these he summarizes in the prologue, v. 1–11, as vanity. He echoes the refrain of *kahal* when he says, "all is vanity."

Koheleth himself enjoyed life. He implies that life is enjoyable, meaningful, and a source of happiness.

Much more is implied than is said openly in Koheleth. God (His essence) is concealed in Elohim. An overwhelming belief in higher values for man is implied in a repetitive description of the futility of the race for wealth and possessions. The limitations of man's understanding are hinted at by a continual emphasis on the importance of and the futility of wisdom. Even the strong religious convictions of a Solomon are concealed by the assumption of the name Koheleth.

ב) הֲבֵל הֲבָלִים אָמַר קֹהֶלֶת הֲבֵל הֲבָלִים הַכֹּל הָבֶל:

(ב) **הבל הבלים אמר קהלת.** קהלת קורא תגר ואומר על כל יצירת שבעת ימי בראשית, שהכל הבל של הבלים הוא: **הבל.** הבל נקוד חטף פתח לפי שהוא דבוק, כלומר הבל שבהבלים. שבעת הבלים כנגד מעשה שבעת ימי בראשית (מדרש תהלים צב: א):

KOHELETH. As stated above, "Koheleth" derives from the word *kahal,* an assembly or collection of people. Since the name is also the title of the book, we might describe Koheleth as a collection of thoughts and philosophical meditations brought together by the author, the . . .

SON OF DAVID. Son of the Psalmist who so perfectly reflected the innermost emotions, feelings and aspirations of man.

KING. As king who was in contact with all his contemporaries; whose reputation as a wise man brought rulers and potentates from all over the world to his palace.

IN JERUSALEM. In the city so many of whose inhabitants were famous for their wisdom; in the city that glorified wisdom.

2] VANITY OF VANITIES . . . ALL IS VANITY. With a bold, seemingly heretical opening statement, Koheleth shocks his audience and wins over the dissidents. In fact, Koheleth echoes the voice of the frustrated members of *kahal* who are overcome by evil and who see only disorder and chaos in the world. In verses 2 and 3 he sums up the thinking of the dissidents — "all is vanity"; "what profit has man of all his labor?"

We know that Koheleth says "all is vanity" with tongue in cheek, for time and again throughout the book he stresses that life is to be enjoyed and that man is held responsible and accountable for all his deeds. Certainly, one who enjoys

2] Vanity of vanities, said Koheleth, vanity of vanities, all is vanity.

life and urges others to enjoy it does not think that life is vanity. But he who sees life only as a race for material possessions cannot find higher values or meaning in living. Such a person sees only inequities among men, monotony and routine in nature, and frustration in the human struggle. To him, all is vanity.

VANITY OF VANITIES. The accepted meanings of the word "vanity" are (a) worthlessness and (b) futility. Worthlessness refers to a situation where the objective is attainable but hardly worth the effort, whereas futility refers to a situation where the objective is impossible of attainment. In the prologue (1–11), where Koheleth gives voice to the thinking of *kahal,* there is little doubt that the first meaning is intended. "All is worthless," says Koheleth, as he dramatically opens his volume with a forceful presentation of blasphemy. But in verse 12 he starts anew in the first person; and in verse 13, which is his first evaluation, he speaks of an Elohim who controls the universe and gives it direction. He weakens the argument of worthlessness and haphazardness.

As we go along in the book we shall see that from time to time Koheleth changes the meaning of vanity from "worthlessness" to "futility" depending on the context. We shall see that Koheleth means at times that it is "futile" for man to try to understand the ways of Elohim. To the limited human mind the vanities must appear as evil, as imperfections in the universe.

3] WHAT PROFIT . . . ? A rhetorical question. There is no profit, nothing to be gained from living. Life has no specific

ג] מַה־יִּתְרוֹן לָאָדָם בְּכָל־עֲמָלוֹ שֶׁיַּעֲמֹל תַּחַת הַשָּׁמֶשׁ:
ד] דּוֹר הֹלֵךְ וְדוֹר בָּא וְהָאָרֶץ לְעוֹלָם עֹמָדֶת:

(ג) **מה יתרון.** שכר ומותר: **תחת השמש.** תמורת התורה, שהיא קרויה אור, שנאמר (משלי ו: כג) ותורה אור — כל עמל שהוא מחליף בו את עסק התורה, מה שכר בו?! (ד) **דור הלך ודור בא.** כל מה שהרשע יגע ועמל לעשוק ולגזול, אינו מבלה את מעשיו, כי הדור הולך ודור אחר בא ונוטל הכל מיד בניו, כענין שנאמר (איוב כ: י) בניו ירצו דלים: **והארץ לעולם עומדת.** ומי הם המתקיימים? הענוים הנמוכים המגיעים עצמם עד לארץ, כענין שנאמר (תהלים לז: יא) וענוים יירשו־ארץ. ומדרש תנחומא אומר: כל צדיקי ישראל נקראו ארץ, שנאמר (מלאכי ג: יב) (ואתם תהיו לי) [כי־תהיו אתם] ארץ חפץ (ע׳ מדרש תהלים לו: יא): (ה) **וזרח**

purpose; all is haphazard. This verse seems to be more forcefully blasphemous than even the preceding one. Yet the Rabbis maintain that this statement is consonant with the basic teachings of religion; it even justifies the inclusion of Koheleth in the Canon. How does one reconcile the obvious contradiction?

UNDER THE SUN. The Rabbis see "under the sun" as the key phrase. Since "under the sun there is no profit," implicitly, then, *above* the sun there is profit.

The blasphemous statements in Koheleth refer to the material world under the sun. If one takes the "under-the-sun" point of view, if he believes only what he sees or understands in the concrete world under the sun, then life's labor has no profit. Life is subject to haphazard natural circumstances. It follows no logical pattern and it is replete with injustice and inequities. Only when man reaches outside of the physical universe, "above the sun," is he able to find meaning in living. Only the spiritual and metaphysical give profit and purpose to living.

Thus, in this blasphemous verse, the Rabbis uncover a fundamental belief of religion. Yet it is derived only by im-

3] What profit has man of all his labor under the sun?

4] One generation passes away, and another generation comes, but the earth abides forever.

plication. It would seem that we are urged here, at the beginning of the book, to look for the hidden meanings in Koheleth. Sometimes there is more to be derived from the inference than from the explicit verse or phrase.

We must repeat that the so-called blasphemy and heresy of Koheleth is not the conviction of King Solomon but the thinking of *kahal* which Koheleth voices. Koheleth echoes the expression of *kahal*; he exaggerates the conclusions to which materialist thinking must lead; he shows the futility of the "under-the-sun" approach.

We, ourselves, may be part of the *kahal* of which and to which Koheleth speaks. It would be difficult to find the person who did not raise in his mind such heretical thoughts at one time or another. Yet even as Solomon allows himself license and freedom of expression, he manages to imply by inference that life does have meaning and purpose; that there is a Providence.

It is of no small significance that the phrase "under the sun" appears no less than 29 times in Koheleth. If we add to this the phrases of similar meaning — "under the heaven" (1:13 and 2:3) and "on earth" (8:16) — we find 32 such phrases in the book. Thus it seems that Koheleth has deliberately scattered these phrases throughout the work to remind us that the heretical verses are not his personal convictions but rather his voicing of the conclusions reached by an "under-the-sun" or "this-worldly" philosophy.

ה) וְזָרַח הַשֶּׁמֶשׁ וּבָא הַשָּׁמֶשׁ וְאֶל־מְקוֹמוֹ שׁוֹאֵף זוֹרֵחַ הוּא שָׁם׃

ו) הוֹלֵךְ אֶל־דָּרוֹם וְסוֹבֵב אֶל־צָפוֹן סוֹבֵב סֹבֵב הוֹלֵךְ הָרוּחַ
וְעַל־סְבִיבֹתָיו שָׁב הָרוּחַ׃

ז) כָּל־הַנְּחָלִים הֹלְכִים אֶל־הַיָּם וְהַיָּם אֵינֶנּוּ מָלֵא אֶל־מְקוֹם
שֶׁהַנְּחָלִים הֹלְכִים שָׁם הֵם שָׁבִים לָלָכֶת׃

ח) כָּל־הַדְּבָרִים יְגֵעִים לֹא־יוּכַל אִישׁ לְדַבֵּר לֹא־תִשְׂבַּע עַיִן
לִרְאוֹת וְלֹא־תִמָּלֵא אֹזֶן מִשְּׁמֹעַ׃

השמש וגו׳ (דור הולך ודור בא). כאשר השמש תזרח שחרית ותשקע ערבית ותלך כל הלילה, שואפת לשוב אל מקום אשר זרחה אתמול משם, שתזרח שם גם היום: (ו) **[הולך] הרוח.** רוחו של שמש, טלנ״ט בלעז (**talant**, will), כמו (יחזקאל א:כ) (אל) [על] אשר יהיה־שם הרוח ללכת: **ועל־סביבתיו שב** גם מחר, כל היקף וסובב שסבב אתמול הוא מקיף וסובב היום: **הולך אל־דרום** לעולם ביום: **וסובב אל־צפון** לעולם בלילה: **סובב סבב** הולך אל־פני מזרח ומערב, שפעמים מהלכתן ביום ופעמים מסבבתן בלילה, בתמוז מהלכתן ובטבת סובבתן (עירובין נו ע״א). אף הרשעים, כל מה ששמשן זורחת — סופן לשקוע; כל מה שהם הולכים ומתגברים — סופם לשוב אל מקום צחנתם; ממקום הטנופת באו, ולמקום הטנופת ילכו. וכן (ז) **כל הנחלים הלכים אל־הים והים איננו מלא,** לפי שאינן נשארים בתוכו, כי ים אוקיינוס הוא גבוה מכל העולם כולו, שנאמר (עמוס ה:ח) הקורא למי־הים וישפכם וגומר, ומהיכן אדם שופך — מלמעלה למטה (בראשית רבה כג:ז; בכורות ט ע״א), והנחלים הולכים במחילות תחת ההרים מאוקיינוס וחוזרים ונובעים, וזהו **אל־מקום שהנחלים הלכים שם הם שבים,** אף הרשע, כל עומת שבא — כן ילך: (ח) **כל־הדברים יגעים וגו׳ לא־תשבע עין... ולא־תמלא אזן.** מוסב על מה יתרון; אם מחליף הוא עסק התורה לדבר דברים בטלים, הרי הם יגעים, ולא יוכל להשיג את כולם; ואם במראית העין בא לעסוק — עינו לא תשבע, ואם בשמיעת האזן — אזנו לא תמלא:

4] One generation passes...another...comes. An expression of utter despair over the short span of human life, over mortality and lack of continuity. The materialist "under-the-sun" philosophy finds no goal or purpose in life, no continuity in history. We live only to die. A generation goes and a generation comes; the cycle ever repeats itself. Only the earth seems to abide forever.

5] The sun rises and the sun sets and strives again to the place from whence it rises.

6] The wind goes to the south and turns to the north; thus round and round the wind goes and returns upon its circuits.

7] All the rivers flow into the sea, yet the sea is not full; unto the place where the rivers go, there they continue to flow.

8] All the things are tiresome; therefore, man cannot speak of them, the eye is not pleased to see, nor the ear filled from hearing.

5] THE SUN RISES AND THE SUN SETS . . .

6] ROUND AND ROUND THE WIND GOES . . .

7] WHERE THE RIVERS GO, THERE THEY CONTINUE . . .

8] THE EYE IS NOT PLEASED . . . NOR THE EAR FILLED . . .

Since the limited human mind becomes bored with what appears as routine, then even the sun, the wind, and the sea are tiresome. The man who does not see beyond the sun, who uncovers no meaning in life or in the phenomena of the physical universe, finds little to speak of once he recognizes their existence. His eye has become accustomed to their monotonous recurrence; his ear, too, has become insensitive to the commonplace and does not enjoy hearing about it.

Were man to possess a mature mind at birth, he would instinctively ask how the sun, the wind, and the sea came about. Born physically helpless and mentally immature, however, man requires many years for full physical and intellectual

ט] מַה־שֶּֽׁהָיָה הוּא שֶׁיִּהְיֶה וּמַה־שֶּׁנַּעֲשָׂה הוּא שֶׁיֵּעָשֶׂה וְאֵין כָּל־
חָדָשׁ תַּחַת הַשָּׁמֶשׁ׃
י] יֵשׁ דָּבָר שֶׁיֹּאמַר רְאֵה־זֶה חָדָשׁ הוּא כְּבָר הָיָה לְעֹלָמִים
אֲשֶׁר הָיָה מִלְּפָנֵנוּ׃
יא] אֵין זִכְרוֹן לָרִאשֹׁנִים וְגַם לָאַחֲרֹנִים שֶׁיִּהְיוּ לֹא־יִהְיֶה לָהֶם
זִכָּרוֹן עִם שֶׁיִּהְיוּ לָאַחֲרֹנָה׃

(ט) **מה־שהיה הוא שיהיה וגומר.** בכל מה שהוא למד בדבר שהוא חליפי השמש אין בו חידוש, לא יראה אלא מה שהיה כבר, שנברא בששת ימי בראשית; אבל ההוגה בתורה מוצא בה תמיד חידושי טעמים, כענין שנאמר (משלי ה: יט) דדיה ירווך בכל־עת — מה הדד הזה, כל זמן שהתינוק ממשמש בו מוצא בו [חלב, אף דברי תורה כל זמן שאדם הוגה בהן מוצא בהן] טעם (עירובין נד ע״ב), וכן מצינו במסכת חגיגה (יד ע״ב) שאמר רבי אלעזר בן (הורקנוס) [ערך] דברים שלא שמעתן אזן במעשה מרכבה: (י) **יש דבר** בא לידך תחת השמש, **שיאמר** לך האומר עליו **ראה־זה** דבר **חדש הוא,** ואינו חדש, שכבר היה בעולמים שעברו לפנינו, אלא (יא) **שאין זכרון לראשנים,** לכך דומה להיות חדש; **וגם לאחרנים** שיהיו לאחרינו **לא־יהיה להם זכרון** בדורות שיהיו **לאחרנה** להם. ומדרש אגדה (ע׳ קה״ר) דורשו כנגד אבוד זכר עמלק, וסופו של זכר אדום למחות, שנאמר (עובדיה א: יח) ולא־יהיה שריד לבית עשו:

development. During this long period of maturation, he is more often than not exposed to materialistic and naturalistic philosophies that rob the most exalted natural phenomena of their meaningfulness, and present them as mere self perpetuating routine.

Just as the "under-the-sun" view finds no meaning in human history, so can it find no revelation in repetitive physical phenomena. The sun, the wind, the rivers and the sea, which have served as a source of inspiration for prophets, poets, and great and imaginative minds, are to the "under-the-sun" mind mere natural realities, in routine motion.

9] THERE IS NOTHING NEW UNDER THE SUN.

9] Only what has been will be, and only what has been done will be done again, and there is nothing new under the sun.

10] Sometimes there is a thing about which one will say, "See, this is new"; but it already existed — in the ages before us.

11] There is no remembrance of the earlier generations; nor will there be remembrance of the later generations by those who come after them.

10] IT ALREADY EXISTED . . .

11] NO REMEMBRANCE OF THE EARLIER GENERATIONS . . .

Life and the physical world are monotonous and habitual; there is little difference between one day and the next. Man and the physical universe will continue to do what they have already done. A mechanistic universe leaves little room for anything new under the sun. Just as the physical phenomena operate out of necessity — they have no free will — so does man operate out of necessity. From the mechanistic point of view, man's behavior and performance are all the result of natural causes. So why remember the *man*? Why glorify him? There was little else he could do but live the way he did.

True, man has invented new machines and tools. This has not changed man. He is just the same intelligent animal. He has improved his living conditions, but he has not improved himself. From the mechanistic point of view, he has no free will and so cannot improve himself morally. In each generation, he is guilty of the same evils and the same iniquities. He operates out of necessity — the victim of the natural forces that control his behavior.

יב] אֲנִי קֹהֶלֶת הָיִיתִי מֶלֶךְ עַל־יִשְׂרָאֵל בִּירוּשָׁלָם׃
יג] וְנָתַתִּי אֶת־לִבִּי לִדְרוֹשׁ וְלָתוּר בַּחָכְמָה עַל כָּל־אֲשֶׁר נַעֲשָׂה
תַּחַת הַשָּׁמָיִם הוּא עִנְיַן רָע נָתַן אֱלֹהִים לִבְנֵי הָאָדָם לַעֲנוֹת
בּוֹ׃

(יב) **אני קהלת הייתי מלך** על כל העולם, ולבסוף על ישראל, ולבסוף על ירושלים לבדה, ולבסוף על מקלי (סנהדרין כ ע״ב), שהרי נאמר, הייתי מלך בירושלם, אבל עכשיו איני מלך: (יג) **ונתתי את לבי לדרוש** בתורה, היא החכמה, ולהתבונן בה על כל המעשה הרע האמור למעלה, הנעשה תחת השמש; ובינותי בה שהוא הענין הרע, אשר נתן הקדוש ברוך הוא לפני בני האדם — (דברים ל:טו) את־החיים ואת־הטוב ואת־המות ואת־הרע: **ענין רע.** מנהג רע להם: **לענות בו.** להתנהג בו: **ענין.** יש לפותרו לשון מעון ודירה, ויש לפותרו לשון עיון ומחשבה, וכן לענות בו: **נתן אלהים.** הניח לפניהם:

12–18 / A quest to understand the evil that Elohim has made

12] I, Koheleth, was king . . . Up to this point, Koheleth has spoken in the third person and presented the conclusions that must follow from a materialistic approach to life. Now he turns to the first person to describe the experiments and observations he made as representative of *kahal* in an objective effort to find meaning in life "under the sun." Koheleth was a king who understood people, who knew that he could not change the thinking of the dissidents until he demonstrated to them by experiment and by logic that their approach led only to purposeless living.

All along Koheleth intersperses phrases and inferences which imply the presence of Providence, of the Creator, in the universe, but he suspends explicit judgment until he has exhausted every effort made by the "under-the-sun" mind to explain all the things that are done.

12] I, Koheleth, was king over Israel in Jerusalem.
13] And I applied myself to search and explore with wisdom, concerning all matters that were done under the heaven — it is an evil thing that Elohim has given man to be afflicted with.

13] IT IS AN EVIL THING . . . From a materialistic point of view it is all evil. The righteous suffer just like the wicked. Life is haphazard and full of frustration.

ELOHIM HAS GIVEN MAN TO BE AFFLICTED WITH. Yet it all comes from Elohim. Nothing happens by itself. Courageously, Koheleth makes his first reference to Elohim in connection with evil. Though evil is the source of man's unhappiness and frustrations, it is also the spur that may lead man to turn to the Almighty for help. And, generally speaking, the dread of evil in the form of punishment is what frequently restrains man from giving vent to all his lower instincts. Were it not for the fear of God, humanity would be devoid of all moral controls.

Nowhere in Koheleth is the revealed name of God, the Tetragrammaton, mentioned. Only the concealed name of God, Elohim, is used. Koheleth, in this verse and throughout the Book of Koheleth, conceals Elohim as the goal even as Elohim is concealed from us in nature.

Elohim conceals himself behind the evil with which He afflicts man. It is man's job to pierce the curtain of evil and to find Elohim. Evil is here to offer a challenge to man. To the extent that man accepts evil graciously and still finds Elohim, to that extent is he to be rewarded.

Though Solomon mentions Elohim forty times in the Book of Koheleth he does not reveal Him as the ultimate goal of man's living until the very end (12:13).

יד] רָאִיתִי אֶת־כָּל־הַמַּעֲשִׂים שֶׁנַּעֲשׂוּ תַּחַת הַשָּׁמֶשׁ וְהִנֵּה הַכֹּל
הֶבֶל וּרְעוּת רוּחַ:
טו] מְעֻוָּת לֹא־יוּכַל לִתְקֹן וְחֶסְרוֹן לֹא־יוּכַל לְהִמָּנוֹת:

(יד) **ורעות רוח**. שבר רוח, כמו (ישעיה ח:ט) רעו עמים וחתו. רוח — טלנ״ט (**talant, spirit**), סוף המעשה בא לידי כאב לב: (טו) **מעות** בחייו

Elohim is the name of God used to indicate that God is the force that created the natural universe. "In the beginning, Elohim created heaven and earth" (Gen. 1:1).

The root words in Hebrew for Elohim are אל meaning *force,* and אלה meaning *these*. The first implies that God is the *force* or source of energy for all creation, and the latter, that all *these* — things in nature — were created by God. Unfortunately, the "under-the-sun" point of view sees only *these* — the concrete things — but not the Creator behind them.

The natural is so much with man that he fails to see the supernatural. The natural is here before him; it is obvious. Therefore, man tends to say "Nature does" or "Nature provides," as though these mechanistic forces rule him and the entire universe. On the other hand, the supernatural has to be searched for and can appear only after much reflection.

This thought is dramatically presented to us in an interesting passage in the Zohar (introductory chapter). The passage, condensed here, is based on a verse in Isaiah (40:26):

שאו מרום עיניכם וראו מי ברא אלה

Lift your eyes on high and see who created these.

Rabbi Shimon said:

> One day I was at the seashore and the prophet Elijah appeared to me and asked me, "Do you know the significance of the words, *Who created these*?"

14] I have seen all the deeds that were done under the sun, and behold, all is vanity and chasing after wind.

15] The crookedness is such as cannot be straightened and the failings so many that they cannot be counted.

> I replied, "No doubt this refers to the heavenly bodies, creations of the Almighty. It is man's duty to study them and thus reveal His glory."
> "There is even a greater secret hidden in these words," said Elijah: "the Hebrew letters for *who* מי and *these* אלה when rearranged spell out Elohim."

If man will always ask "Who?" when he sees "these"; if man will look up to the heavens and ask, "Who created these?" then Elohim will reveal Himself to man. To be satisfied with just seeing "these," to be content with mere outward manifestations and not to ask "Who?" created these, leads man to attribute power and government to haphazard and indifferent forces. This was implicit in the sin of the Jews who bowed down to the golden calf and said, "*These* are your gods, O Israel."

It is man's duty always to ask "Who?" Who is responsible for the universe? Who created life, the human mind, the human spirit? Who rules over the destiny of the people? Who is the source of all the good and all the evil?

14] UNDER THE SUN . . . If nature is the ultimate, however, then "all is vanity." Nature is indifferent to human desire and suffering. To seek meaning in nature itself is as futile as to chase after wind.

15] CROOKEDNESS . . . CANNOT BE STRAIGHTENED. As much as we try to find a consistent pattern in nature, there are

טז) דִּבַּרְתִּי אֲנִי עִם־לִבִּי לֵאמֹר אֲנִי הִנֵּה הִגְדַּלְתִּי וְהוֹסַפְתִּי
חָכְמָה עַל כָּל־אֲשֶׁר־הָיָה לְפָנַי עַל־יְרוּשָׁלִָם וְלִבִּי רָאָה
הַרְבֵּה חָכְמָה וָדָעַת׃
יז) וָאֶתְּנָה לִבִּי לָדַעַת חָכְמָה וְדַעַת הֹלֵלוֹת וְשִׂכְלוּת יָדַעְתִּי
שֶׁגַּם־זֶה הוּא רַעְיוֹן רוּחַ׃
יח) כִּי בְּרֹב חָכְמָה רָב־כָּעַס וְיוֹסִיף דַּעַת יוֹסִיף מַכְאוֹב׃

לא־יוכל לתקן משמת, מי שטרח בערב שבת יאכל בשבת (עבודה זרה ג ע״א, ע״ש); ורבותינו פירשו על הבא על הערוה והוליד ממזר או על תלמיד חכם הפורש מן התורה, שהיה ישר מתחילתו ונתעוות (חגיגה ט ע״א): **וחסרון לא־יוכל להמנות.** זה שחיסר עצמו ממנין הכשרים, לא יוכל להמנות עמהם בקבול שכרם: (טז) **דברתי אני עם־לבי.** עכשיו שירדתי מגדולתי אני נותן לבי לאמר, מי יאמר עלי שאבוא לידי מידה זו: **אני הנה הגדלתי וגומר** (יז) **ואתנה** עכשיו את **לבי לדעת** את טיב **החכמה** מה סופה ואת טיב **ההוללות והסכלות.** הוללות — שיעמום וטירוף הדעת, לשון ערבוב כמו (ישעיה א:כב) מהול במים, וסכלות — שטות. **ידעתי** עתה, **שגם** החכמה יש בו שבר רוח, (יח) **כי ברב החכמה** אדם סומך על רוב חכמתו ואינו מתרחק מן האסור **ובא רב־כעס** להקדוש ברוך הוא: אני אמרתי ארבה סוסים, ולא אשיב את העם מצרימה — ובסוף השיבותי; אני אמרתי ארבה נשים, ולא יסור לבבי — והרי נכתב עלי (מלכים א׳ יא:ד) נשיו הטו אל־לבבו (סנהדרין כא ע״ב); וכן הוא אומר, שעל רוב חכמתו הוא סמך ועשה כמה דברים, שנאמר (משלי ל:א) נאם הגבר לאיתיאל לאיתיאל ואכל (תנחומא וארא ה):

always such profound deviations from the norms set by the logical mind as to make reconciliation impossible.

FAILINGS SO MANY . . . THEY CANNOT BE COUNTED. Likewise, there are so many inequities in nature, especially in the distribution of reward and punishment, that it would be impossible to enumerate them.

16] INCREASED IN WISDOM . . . Koheleth tells us here that his basic approach to find meaning in the universe was through wisdom. He would use rational thinking alone before attempting to explore combinations and other ways of living.

16] I said to myself, I have grown and increased in wisdom over all who preceded me in Jerusalem, and my mind has perceived much wisdom and knowledge.

17] And I have permitted my mind to apply itself to wisdom and to madness and foolishness, even though I knew that this, too, was chasing after wind.

18] For greater use of wisdom only brings on greater vexation, and increased knowledge only leads to greater pain.

17] WISDOM . . . MADNESS AND FOOLISHNESS. Koheleth not only applied wisdom, but he also tried to understand madness and even foolishness as an approach to overcome the purposelessness and suffering in daily living.

EVEN THOUGH I KNEW . . . Though Koheleth knew the futility of grasping the ways of God with the limited human mind, albeit the greatest mind, in order to convince *ḳahal* he was going to try again.

18] GREATER USE OF WISDOM . . . There is little need to explain why foolishness and madness are not satisfactory approaches to living, but even the intellectual approach is bound to be disappointing. In fact, the greater the intellect the greater the vexation. For as man's understanding grows so does his sensitivity to all that is unfair or illogical in the universe. The wider one's experience, the profounder one's thinking, the more apt he is to sense injustice and therefore to suffer greater pain.

Chapter 2

CONTENTMENT

Who is rich?
He who rejoices in his portion.

Talmud

א] אָמַרְתִּי אֲנִי בְּלִבִּי לְכָה־נָּא אֲנַסְּכָה בְשִׂמְחָה וּרְאֵה בְטוֹב
וְהִנֵּה גַם־הוּא הָבֶל׃

ב] לִשְׂחוֹק אָמַרְתִּי מְהוֹלָל וּלְשִׂמְחָה מַה־זֹּה עֹשָׂה׃

ג] תַּרְתִּי בְלִבִּי לִמְשׁוֹךְ בַּיַּיִן אֶת־בְּשָׂרִי וְלִבִּי נֹהֵג בַּחָכְמָה
וְלֶאֱחֹז בְּסִכְלוּת עַד אֲשֶׁר אֶרְאֶה אֵי־זֶה טוֹב לִבְנֵי הָאָדָם
אֲשֶׁר יַעֲשׂוּ תַּחַת הַשָּׁמַיִם מִסְפַּר יְמֵי חַיֵּיהֶם׃

ד] הִגְדַּלְתִּי מַעֲשָׂי בָּנִיתִי לִי בָּתִּים נָטַעְתִּי לִי כְּרָמִים׃

(א) **אמרתי אני בלבי.** הואיל וכן הוא, אחדל לי מן החכמה ואעסוק במשתה תמיד: **אנסכה.** לשון מסך יין לשתות, כמו (משלי ט: ב) מסכה יינה, עירוב יין במים לתקנו או עירוב בשמים ביין לקונדיטון: **וראה בטוב.** כמו וראות בטוב: **והנה גם־הוא הבל.** שהרי ראיתי בנבואה שהרבה קלקולים באים מתוך שחוק: בלשצר מת מתוך משתה, אנשי דור המבול נשטפו מתוך רוב טובה שהשפעת להם: (ב) **לשחוק אמרתי מהולל.** מעורבת בבכי ואנחה: **ולשמחה מה־זה** טובה עושה, הרי סופה תוגה: (ג) **תרתי בלבי.** חזרתי לתור בלבי להחזיק בכולן — במשתה, בחכמה ובסכלות, ולמשוך ולעדן במשתה היין **את־בשרי.** כל סעודת עונג קרוייה על שם היין: **ולבי נהג בחכמה.** אף אם בשרי נמשך ביין, לבי מתגלגל בחכמה, להחזיק בתורה, **ולאחז בסכלות.** בדברים הדומים לי לסכלות, שאמרתי עליהם (משלי ל: א) לאיתיאל ואכל, וכגון לבישת שעטנז וכלאי הכרם שהשטן משיב עליהם ואומות העולם משיבין עליהם; וכן הוא אומר (להלן ז: יח) טוב אשר תאחז בזה וגו׳ (וע׳ רש״י שם); וגם על שאול שנדמה בעיניו סכלות להרוג מאיש (ועד) [עד־] אשה, מעלל ועד־יונק (שמואל א׳ טו: ג; וע׳ יומא כב ע״ב), והיא מצות המקום, וקורא אותה סכלות: (ד) **הגדלתי מעשי** בימי גדולתי:

1–13 / Wisdom, madness, foolishness, good times — which has the greatest meaning for life?

1] Come, i'll try . . . Koheleth proceeds to describe some of the experiments he performed as a representative of the materialist approach to life. In verses 1–2 he gives us a preview of his conclusions.

CHAPTER TWO

1] I said to myself, come, I will try you out with joy and good times — but this, too, was vanity.

2] About laughter I concluded — it is folly; and about joy — what does it accomplish?

3] I explored means of pampering my flesh with wine, acting with wisdom, and at the same time holding on to foolishness — until I could determine which of these is better for men to pursue the few days of their lives under the heavens.

4] I increased my activities; I built myself houses and planted vineyards.

2] WHAT DOES IT ACCOMPLISH? Alas, joy and good times do not bring lasting satisfaction in their wake. They help man forget his troubles for the moment. But after the sensual pleasures, what? Life must have some purpose, some meaning more enduring than the joy of the moment.

People who are concerned only with having a good time are usually bored and fed up with life. They have no spiritual source to revitalize their being and to fill their better moments. The pleasure-seeker is unhappy if he doesn't get what he wants; and when he gets it he is bored. There are too many voids in his life.

3] PAMPERING MY FLESH WITH WINE . . . Now Koheleth goes on to describe in detail, in the following verses, how he reached the above conclusions. He actually supplied himself with the ingredients of the worldly "good life" in order to determine whether these would bring happiness.

ה] עָשִׂיתִי לִי גַּנּוֹת וּפַרְדֵּסִים וְנָטַעְתִּי בָהֶם עֵץ כָּל־פֶּרִי:
ו] עָשִׂיתִי לִי בְּרֵכוֹת מָיִם לְהַשְׁקוֹת מֵהֶם יַעַר צוֹמֵחַ עֵצִים:
ז] קָנִיתִי עֲבָדִים וּשְׁפָחוֹת וּבְנֵי־בַיִת הָיָה לִי גַּם מִקְנֶה בָקָר
וָצֹאן הַרְבֵּה הָיָה לִי מִכֹּל שֶׁהָיוּ לְפָנַי בִּירוּשָׁלִָם:
ח] כָּנַסְתִּי לִי גַּם־כֶּסֶף וְזָהָב וּסְגֻלַּת מְלָכִים וְהַמְּדִינוֹת עָשִׂיתִי
לִי שָׁרִים וְשָׁרוֹת וְתַעֲנֻגוֹת בְּנֵי הָאָדָם שִׁדָּה וְשִׁדּוֹת:
ט] וְגָדַלְתִּי וְהוֹסַפְתִּי מִכֹּל שֶׁהָיָה לְפָנַי בִּירוּשָׁלִָם אַף חָכְמָתִי
עָמְדָה לִּי:
י] וְכֹל אֲשֶׁר שָׁאֲלוּ עֵינַי לֹא אָצַלְתִּי מֵהֶם לֹא־מָנַעְתִּי אֶת־לִבִּי
מִכָּל־שִׂמְחָה כִּי־לִבִּי שָׂמֵחַ מִכָּל־עֲמָלִי וְזֶה־הָיָה חֶלְקִי
מִכָּל־עֲמָלִי:
יא] וּפָנִיתִי אֲנִי בְּכָל־מַעֲשַׂי שֶׁעָשׂוּ יָדַי וּבֶעָמָל שֶׁעָמַלְתִּי לַעֲשׂוֹת
וְהִנֵּה הַכֹּל הֶבֶל וּרְעוּת רוּחַ וְאֵין יִתְרוֹן תַּחַת הַשָּׁמֶשׁ:

(ה) **עץ כל־פרי.** שהיה שלמה מכיר בחכמתו את גידי הארץ, איזה גיד הולך אל כוש — ונטע בו פלפלין, איזה הולך לארץ חרובי — ונטע בו חרובין, שכל גידי הארצות באים לציון שמשם משתיתו של עולם, שנאמר (תהלים נ:ב) מציון מכלל־יפי; לכך נאמר עץ כל פרי. במדרש תנחומא (קדושים י): (ו) **ברכות מים.** כמין ביברים של דגים שחופרין בקרקע: (ח) **וסגלת מלכים.** גנזי מלכים, זהב וכסף ואבן יקרה, שהמלכים מסגלים בגנזיהם: **והמדינות.** סגולת כל סוחרים: **שרים ושרות.** מיני כלי זמר: **שדה ושדות.** מרכבות נוי, עגלות צב; ובלשון תלמוד יש (שבת קכ ע״א) שידה תיבה ומגדל: (ט) **אף חכמתי.** גם חכמתי לא הנחתי בשביל כל המעשים האלה, ועמדה לי. ולא שכחתיה. דבר אחר, **עמדה לי** — לעזרה מכל אלה: (י) **לא אצלתי.** לא רחקתי להבדל מהם; וכן (במדבר יא:כה) ויאצל מן־הרוח [אשר עליו] ויתן על... הזקנים, כמנורה שמדליקין ממנה נרות הרבה ואין אורה חסר כלום (ע״ש תויב״ע; וע׳ רש״י שם יא:יז מהספרי): **וזה־היה חלקי.** ואחרי עשותי כל אלה, אין לי מכולם אלא זה; רב ושמואל: חד אמר מקלו וחד אמר קידו, מקידה של חרש ששותין בה (סנהדרין כ ע״ב, וע״ש). ויש פותרים במדרש אגדה (ע׳ קה״ר) כל הענין בבתי מדרשות ותלמידים ובבתי כנסיות; **יער צומח עצים.** עמי הארץ למלאכת שדות וכרמים: (יא) **ופניתי** עתה **בכל־מעשי** ורואה אני שאין יתרון בהם, כי מכולם אני חסר:

10] AND THAT WAS MY REWARD . . . The temporary satisfac-

5] I made me gardens and orchards and planted in them every kind of fruit tree.

6] I made me pools of water to irrigate therefrom a forest of trees.

7] I acquired menservants and maidservants and I had caretakers of the house. I also possessed more cattle, both herd and flock, than anyone who preceded me in Jerusalem.

8] I also assembled silver and gold and treasures of kings and the provinces. I acquired singers and songstresses — the delights of people, a variety of chariots.

9] I grew great in wealth and surpassed all who had preceded me in Jerusalem. Even my wisdom stood me in good stead in this effort.

10] And whatever my eyes desired, I did not deny them. I did not deprive myself of any pleasure — for my heart rejoiced in all my labor, and that was my reward for all my labor.

11] Then I looked on all the works that my hands had wrought and on the labor I had performed, and behold, all is vanity and striving after wind, and there is no profit for man under the sun.

tion of accumulation and possession; the temporary feeling of security.

11] THEN I LOOKED ON ALL THE WORKS . . . When one is absorbed in the all-consuming rat race to accumulate wealth, there is little time for reflection. Most materially aggressive

יב] וּפָנִיתִי אֲנִי לִרְאוֹת חָכְמָה וְהוֹלֵלוֹת וְסִכְלוּת כִּי מֶה הָאָדָם
שֶׁיָּבוֹא אַחֲרֵי הַמֶּלֶךְ אֵת אֲשֶׁר־כְּבָר עָשׂוּהוּ׃
יג] וְרָאִיתִי אָנִי שֶׁיֵּשׁ יִתְרוֹן לַחָכְמָה מִן־הַסִּכְלוּת כִּיתְרוֹן הָאוֹר
מִן־הַחֹשֶׁךְ׃

(יב) ופניתי אני לראות חכמה. פונה אני מכל עסקי להתבונן בתורה, **והוללות וסכלות** — עונש עבירות, **כי מה האדם שיבוא אחרי המלך** להתחנן לו על גזירה שגזרו עליו, וכבר עשאוהו למעשה הגזירה לגוזרה; טוב לו להתבונן תחילה במעשיו, ולא יצטרך לבקש: **(יג) מן־הסכלות.** הוא הרשע:

people never find time for reflection. But the wise man takes time out to look back on all his works. He asks "Why?" What has he achieved by accumulating all this wealth? Has it brought him happiness? If he could be happier with less, and apparently some people are, then why has he wasted so much valuable time in the pursuit of wealth?

Koheleth, after reflection, states that all this wealth has not made him any happier. It has not brought greater meaning to life. It is but vanity and a striving after wind.

12] At the same time . . . In all the time he spent accumulating wealth, Koheleth had ample opportunity to evaluate wisdom, madness and foolishness as sources of happiness. In verse 2, above, he has practically disposed of madness and

12] At the same time, I evaluated wisdom, madness, and foolishness — for of what value is the man who would come after the king to perform an experiment that had already been performed by the king?

13] I concluded that the advantage of wisdom over foolishness was like the advantage of light over darkness.

foolishness. And in the next verse he tells us that wisdom is in a class by itself.

OF WHAT VALUE IS THE MAN . . . Koheleth has already intimated, in verses 1 and 2 above, the conclusions of the experiment. Now, parenthetically, he states that it would not be profitable for the ordinary man to repeat the experiment. Even if he should be a wise individual, he is not likely to have the vast resources of a Solomon at his disposal. Koheleth assures him that even the great wealth of a king and the wisdom of a Solomon cannot of themselves add meaning to life.

13] LIKE THE ADVANTAGE OF LIGHT OVER DARKNESS. Darkness is naught, the absence of light; it is incomparable to light. So is foolishness incomparable to wisdom.

יד] הֶחָכָם עֵינָיו בְּרֹאשׁוֹ וְהַכְּסִיל בַּחֹשֶׁךְ הוֹלֵךְ וְיָדַעְתִּי גַם־אָנִי
שֶׁמִּקְרֶה אֶחָד יִקְרֶה אֶת־כֻּלָּם׃
טו] וְאָמַרְתִּי אֲנִי בְּלִבִּי כְּמִקְרֵה הַכְּסִיל גַּם־אֲנִי יִקְרֵנִי וְלָמָּה
חָכַמְתִּי אֲנִי אָז יֹתֵר וְדִבַּרְתִּי בְלִבִּי שֶׁגַּם־זֶה הָבֶל׃
טז] כִּי אֵין זִכְרוֹן לֶחָכָם עִם־הַכְּסִיל לְעוֹלָם בְּשֶׁכְּבָר הַיָּמִים
הַבָּאִים הַכֹּל נִשְׁכָּח וְאֵיךְ יָמוּת הֶחָכָם עִם־הַכְּסִיל׃
יז] וְשָׂנֵאתִי אֶת־הַחַיִּים כִּי רַע עָלַי הַמַּעֲשֶׂה שֶׁנַּעֲשָׂה תַּחַת הַשָּׁמֶשׁ
כִּי־הַכֹּל הֶבֶל וּרְעוּת רוּחַ׃

(יד) [החכם] **עיניו בראשו.** בתחילת הדבר מסתכל מה יהא בסופו: **וידעתי גם־אני.** גם אני (ידעתי), אשר משבח את החכם מן הכסיל, יודע (אני) ששניהם ימותו: **ואמרתי אני בלבי** וגומר. כלומר, לפי ששניהם מתים, שמא אהרהר בלבי מעתה, **כמקרה** הרשע **גם־אני יקרני,** ולמה אהיה צדיק **אז יתר? ודברתי בלבי,** שאם אהרהר כן — הבל הוא, (טז) **כי אין זכרון** החכם והכסיל שוין, אחרי מותן לא ייזכרו שניהם יחד, שזה — זכרונו לטובה, וזה — זכרונו לרעה: **בשכבר הימים הבאים הכל נשכח.** בשביל אשר אני רואה את הרשעים אשר היו כבר והצליחו מאד, ובימים הבאים אחריהם נשכחה כל גבורתם והצלחתם; **ואיך ימות החכם עם־הכסיל.** אני רואה הצדיקים מצליחים במיתתם ומועילים לבניהם, כגון (ויקרא כו: מב) וזכרתי (אני) את, בריתי יעקוב וגומר, (ירמיה ב: ב) זכרתי לך חסד נעוריך: (יז) **ושנאתי את־החיים.** שהיה מתנבא על דורו של רחבעם, שהיו רשעים:

14–17 / Is wisdom in itself the goal to be sought?

14] ARE IN HIS HEAD . . . The wise man and the fool both see. However, the wise man does not rush to act merely on the basis of what he sees. What his eyes see is first evaluated

14] The wise man's eyes are in his head; whereas the fool walks in darkness. And yet I know that one fate will befall them both.

15] I said to myself: If whatever befalls the fool will also befall me, then why do I strive to become wiser? I concluded that this, too, is vanity.

16] The wise man, just like the fool, will not be remembered forever. When the days pass all will be forgotten, even the fact that the wise man dies just like the fool.

17] I hated life; it grieved me to see what was done under the sun; all is vanity and chasing after wind.

by his head. The wise man learns from experience and thus develops a rich background. It is in the light of this rich background that he evaluates what he sees. The fool, on the other hand, is easily misled by what he sees and, because he does not evaluate, plunges forward in darkness.

ONE FATE WILL BEFALL . . . In spite of his high regard for wisdom, Koheleth takes cognizance of the popular grievance that there seems to be no difference in the lot of the wise man such as to give him any material advantage over the fool.

יח) וְשָׂנֵאתִי אֲנִי אֶת־כָּל־עֲמָלִי שֶׁאֲנִי עָמֵל תַּחַת הַשָּׁמֶשׁ שֶׁאַנִּיחֶנּוּ
לָאָדָם שֶׁיִּהְיֶה אַחֲרָי׃
יט) וּמִי יוֹדֵעַ הֶחָכָם יִהְיֶה אוֹ סָכָל וְיִשְׁלַט בְּכָל־עֲמָלִי שֶׁעָמַלְתִּי
וְשֶׁחָכַמְתִּי תַּחַת הַשָּׁמֶשׁ גַּם־זֶה הָבֶל׃
כ) וְסַבּוֹתִי אֲנִי לְיַאֵשׁ אֶת־לִבִּי עַל כָּל־הֶעָמָל שֶׁעָמַלְתִּי תַּחַת
הַשָּׁמֶשׁ׃
כא) כִּי־יֵשׁ אָדָם שֶׁעֲמָלוֹ בְּחָכְמָה וּבְדַעַת וּבְכִשְׁרוֹן וּלְאָדָם שֶׁלֹּא
עָמַל־בּוֹ יִתְּנֶנּוּ חֶלְקוֹ גַּם־זֶה הֶבֶל וְרָעָה רַבָּה׃

(יט) **גם־זה הבל.** גם זה אחד מן ההבלים שנבראו בעולם, שהחכם יגע והכסיל יורשו: (כ) **וסבותי אני ליאש.** שלא ליגע ולעמול: (כא) **כי־יש אדם.** כמשמעו כפשוטו; ומדרש אגדה בתנחומא (תנחומא ב׳, בראשית לד) מכנהו כלפי הקדוש ברוך הוא, שנאמר בו (יחזקאל א: כו) ועל דמות הכסא דמות כמראה אדם: **שעמלו בחכמה.** שנאמר (משלי ג:יט) ה׳ בחכמה יסד־ארץ, [**ובדעת,** שנאמר] (שם ג:כ) בדעתו תהומות נבקעו, ולבריות שלא עמלו בו נתן חלק בו: **גם־זה הבל ורעה רבה.** והם נעשו דור של הבל, ורבה רעת האדם בארץ בדור המבול (ע׳ קה״ר):

18–21 / Labor for the next generation?

18] FOR I SHALL HAVE TO LEAVE IT . . . True, wisdom in itself brings no material advantage. But materialism in itself is even more disappointing. The materialist is overcome with despair when he reflects that he has to ultimately part with his wealth. Even the fact that his wealth will be inherited by

18] And I despised the wealth that I labor for under the sun, for I shall have to leave it to a man who will succeed me.

19] And who knows whether he will be a wise man or a fool? Yet he will rule over all the wealth for which I have labored and planned. This, too, is vanity.

20] I worked myself into a state of despair in regard to all the wealth for which I labored under the sun.

21] For if a man should work with wisdom, knowledge and skill, and have to leave his wealth to one who did not labor for it — it is vanity and great evil.

his children does not console the materialist. On the contrary, the possibility that his children may destroy that wealth only increases his anguish. In some cases his greed is so overwhelming that the materialist not only cannot bear the thought that he must eventually part with his wealth, but he also begrudges it his own children — because they did not labor for the wealth.

כב] כִּי מֶה־הֹוֶה לָאָדָם בְּכָל־עֲמָלוֹ וּבְרַעְיוֹן לִבּוֹ שֶׁהוּא עָמֵל
תַּחַת הַשָּׁמֶשׁ:
כג] כִּי כָל־יָמָיו מַכְאֹבִים וָכַעַס עִנְיָנוֹ גַּם־בַּלַּיְלָה לֹא־שָׁכַב
לִבּוֹ גַּם־זֶה הֶבֶל הוּא:

(כב) כי מה־הוה וגומר. כי מה מותר הוה לאדם בכל־עמלו ושברון לבו, בעמל ודאגה שהוא עמל ומניח לאחרים ? (כג) ענינו. מנהגו ; גם זה אחד מן ההבלים הנוהגים בעולם:

22–23 / Labor for the accumulation of wealth?

22] What good does a man derive . . . If labor has no goal or purpose "under the sun," if man labors all his life and does not attain happiness, if man's labor and accumulated

22] What good does a man derive from all his labor
and his planning to accumulate wealth under
the sun?
23] All his days bring pain and anger as his lot.
Even at night he has no peace of mind. This,
too, is vanity.

wealth is taken from him and handed to another — who did not work for it — then such labor leads only to despair.

23] All his days bring pain . . . Why should a man subject himself to endless toil? Why should a man suffer so much pain, be beset all his life with problems, and spend sleepless nights to accumulate wealth, when he has not time to enjoy it and must pass it on to another who did not labor for it?

כד] אֵין־טוֹב בָּאָדָם שֶׁיֹּאכַל וְשָׁתָה וְהֶרְאָה אֶת־נַפְשׁוֹ טוֹב
בַּעֲמָלוֹ גַּם־זֹה רָאִיתִי אָנִי כִּי מִיַּד הָאֱלֹהִים הִיא׃
כה] כִּי מִי יֹאכַל וּמִי יָחוּשׁ חוּץ מִמֶּנִּי׃
כו] כִּי לְאָדָם שֶׁטּוֹב לְפָנָיו נָתַן חָכְמָה וְדַעַת וְשִׂמְחָה וְלַחוֹטֶא נָתַן
עִנְיָן לֶאֱסוֹף וְלִכְנוֹס לָתֵת לְטוֹב לִפְנֵי הָאֱלֹהִים גַּם־זֶה הֶבֶל
וּרְעוּת רוּחַ׃

(כד) **אין־טוב באדם.** בתמיה, **שיאכל ושתה והראה את־נפשו טוב.** כלומר, יתן לבו לעשות משפט וצדקה עם המאכל והמשתה; וכן נאמר ליהויקים (ירמיה כב: טו) אביך הלוא אכל ושתה ועשה משפט וצדקה אז טוב לו: (כה) **כי מי יאכל וגו׳.** למה לא אשמח בחלקי במאכל ומשתה? מי ראוי לאכול את יגיעי, ומי ימהר לבולעה מבלעדי? **חוץ ממני.** מבלעדי. זו מדת הרשעים היא, שאוספים לצורך האחרים: (כו) **כי לאדם שטוב לפניו.** לפני האלהים, הנזכר למעלה (פס׳ כד) כי מיד האלהים (הוא) [היא], **נתן חכמה ודעת ושמחה.** לב לעסוק בתורה ובמצוות ולשמוח בחלקו במאכל ובמשתה וכסות נקייה: **ולחוטא נתן ענין** — מנהג, דאגה, **לאסוף והכנוס לתת לטוב לפני האלהים,** כענין שנאמר (אסתר ח: ב) ותשם אסתר את־מרדכי על־בית המן (ע׳ מגילה י ע״ב): **גם זה** אחד מן ההבלים שנתנו לבריות — שהם עמלים ואחר נוטל:

24–26 / The only solution

24] There is no other good for man than to eat and drink . . . From his disillusionment in regard to wealth and worldly pleasures, expressed in the above verses, one might assume that Koheleth would recommend a life of poverty and abstinence from pleasure. However, such self-denial is far from Koheleth's personal philosophy, as he states in verse 25. On the contrary, Koheleth avers that man should eat, drink, and enjoy life. Koheleth only objects to wealth and pleasure as ends in themselves. There must be higher values which wealth and pleasure subserve.

Show himself content with his wealth . . . Man's task is to be content with his wealth. The desire for more only

24] There is no other good for man than to eat and drink and to show himself content with his wealth. This too, I concluded, is a gift of Elohim.
25] For who has consumed delicacies and participated in sensual pleasures more than I?
26] He has given this wisdom and knowledge and,

diminishes or destroys the enjoyment of what one already possesses. Whether they be large or small, man must count his blessings and appreciate them. These blessings may be in the form of health, family, possessions or surroundings — any or all of these. Man should recognize these bounties as gifts of Elohim.

25] WHO . . . PARTICIPATED IN . . . PLEASURES MORE THAN I? A parenthetical remark. Koheleth tells us that we need not be amazed by his "eat, drink and be merry" approach to life, as expressed in the preceding verse. His own life having been one of maximum enjoyment of living, he could justly ask, "Who has participated in sensual pleasures more than I?"

Koheleth looked upon all his talents and all his bounties as gifts of Elohim. He counted his blessings and continually expressed his gratitude to Elohim for them. His delight in wisdom, his enchantment in the discovery of the secrets of nature, his maximal enjoyment of worldly pleasures, all added meaning to life for they were all seen as gifts of Elohim. Koheleth looked upon his great wealth not as an end in itself, but as a means of serving Elohim and of expressing his gratitude to Him.

26] HE HAS GIVEN THIS WISDOM . . .TO THE MAN WHO IS GOOD . . . *Elohim* rewards the good man by giving him this

> therefore, happiness to the man who is good in His eyes; however, to the sinner He has given the thought to gather and accumulate wealth in order to give it away ultimately to him that is good in the sight of Elohim. This, too, is vanity and chasing of wind.

wisdom, the thought (expressed in v. 24) that man should content himself with his portion. It is the secret of happiness. It is the only way to overcome envy and greed, which are the sources of man's unhappiness.

HE HAS GIVEN THE THOUGHT TO GATHER AND ACCUMULATE . . . The sinner, on the other hand, is punished by being given the thought to participate in an endless rat race in the pursuit of wealth. The more he has, the more he desires. At every stage he is not happy with his lot, because he sees more opportunity for gathering and accumulating. Thus a whole life may be wasted in pursuing but never enjoying happiness.

THIS, TOO, IS VANITY . . . Even from a materialistic point of view, man should take time out to enjoy his possessions. His greed for money should not be permitted to enslave man. For even if the thought to accumulate wealth is planted in the brain of the sinner, he still possesses the freedom to reject it. He should be able to see that total preoccupation with moneymaking is complete enslavement. Failure to recognize this, failure to pause for reflection, for the enjoyment of living, is to make of life — vanity and the chasing of wind.

Chapter 3

GOOD AND EVIL

Happy is the man whom you discipline,
O Lord,
and whom you teach out of your law.

Psalms

א] לַכֹּל זְמָן וְעֵת לְכָל־חֵפֶץ תַּחַת הַשָּׁמָיִם:
ב] עֵת לָלֶדֶת וְעֵת לָמוּת עֵת לָטַעַת וְעֵת לַעֲקוֹר נָטוּעַ:
ג] עֵת לַהֲרוֹג וְעֵת לִרְפּוֹא עֵת לִפְרוֹץ וְעֵת לִבְנוֹת:
ד] עֵת לִבְכּוֹת וְעֵת לִשְׂחוֹק עֵת סְפוֹד וְעֵת רְקוֹד:

(א) **לכל זמן.** אל ישמח האוסף בהון מהבל, כי אם עכשיו הוא בידו עוד יירשוהו צדיקים; אלא שעדיין לא הגיע הזמן, כי לכל דבר יש זמן קבוע מתי יהיה: **לכל־חפץ.** לכל דבר. כל הדברים קרויים חפצים בלשון משנה: (ב) **עת ללדת.** לתשעה חדשים; **ועת למות.** קצב שנות של כל דור ודור: **עת לטעת** גוי וממלכה; **ועת לעקור.** עת יבא להעקר: (ג) **עת להרוג** אומה שלימה כשמגיע יום פקודתה, כמו שנאמר (ישעיה יד: ל) ושאריתך יהרג; **ועת לרפוא** שברם, כענין שנאמר במצרים (שם יט: כב) ושבו עד־ה׳ ונעתר להם ורפאם: **עת לפרוץ** חומת העיר, כשנגזר עליה, שנאמר (נחמיה א: ג) וחומת ירושלם מפורצת; **ועת לבנות.** שאמר (עמוס ט: יא) ובניתיה כימי עולם: (ד) **עת לבכות.** בתשעה באב; **ועת לשחוק.** לעתיד לבא, שנאמר (תהלים קכו: ב) אז

1–9 / Good and evil are shared by all

1] For all things there is a season . . . In the first chapter, Koheleth pointed out that a naturalistic philosophy has no meaningful import for life; man must seek out the supernatural. Chapter Two emphasized that a supernatural approach, plus the realization that one should rejoice in one's portion, leads to happiness. Koheleth now turns to the problem of evil.

Some people believe that evil, or an unusual dose of evil, befalls only them and that their neighbors escape evil. Koheleth assures us that this is not true. Good and evil visit everyone, rich or poor, righteous or wicked. Some seem to get more good and some seem to get more evil. The way Elohim apportions these is beyond human comprehension. But some

1] For all things there is a season, and there is a time for everything under the heavens.

2] There is a time to give birth and there is a time to die; a time to plant and a time to uproot the planted.

3] There is a time to kill and a time to heal; a time to wreck and a time to build.

4] There is a time to weep and a time to laugh; a time to mourn and a time to dance.

good and some evil is the lot of each and every person. For there is a season for everything. Man cannot avoid evil, try as he may.

2] A TIME TO GIVE BIRTH . . . A happy moment, though the Rabbis tell us that no sooner is a man born than he is on the road to death.

A TIME TO DIE. Death produces the greatest sorrow, but it does not discriminate between rich and poor. Thus, the most dreaded evil is shared by everyone.

A TIME TO PLANT . . . Creativity is a great joy; it is a good available to all.

A TIME TO UPROOT . . . There are frustrating times when one must destroy what one has planted. But such frustrations are common to all regardless of financial status.

3] A TIME TO KILL . . . Unnatural death and accident do not discriminate between rich and poor, even as natural death does not.

ה] עֵת לְהַשְׁלִיךְ אֲבָנִים וְעֵת כְּנוֹס אֲבָנִים עֵת לַחֲבוֹק וְעֵת
לִרְחֹק מֵחַבֵּק:

ו] עֵת לְבַקֵּשׁ וְעֵת לְאַבֵּד עֵת לִשְׁמוֹר וְעֵת לְהַשְׁלִיךְ:

ז] עֵת לִקְרוֹעַ וְעֵת לִתְפּוֹר עֵת לַחֲשׁוֹת וְעֵת לְדַבֵּר:

ח] עֵת לֶאֱהֹב וְעֵת לִשְׂנֹא עֵת מִלְחָמָה וְעֵת שָׁלוֹם:

ט] מַה־יִּתְרוֹן הָעוֹשֶׂה בַּאֲשֶׁר הוּא עָמֵל:

ימלא שחוק פינו: **עת ספוד**. בימי אבל; **עת רקוד**. בחתנים וכלות: **(ה) עת להשליך אבנים**. בחורי ישראל מושלכים, (איכה ד:א) תשתפכנה אבני־קדש; **ועת כנוס** אותם מן הגולה (זכריה ט:טז) והושיעם ה׳ אלהיהם ביום ההוא כצאן עמו כי אבני־נזר מתנוססות על־אדמתו: **עת לחבוק** — (ירמיה יג:יא) כי כאשר ידבק האזור וגומר; **ועת לרחק מחבק** — (ישעיה ו:יב) ורחק ה׳ את האדם: **(ו) עת לבקש**. כענין שנאמר (יחזקאל לד:טז) את־האבדת אבקש, לענין נדחי ישראל; **ועת לאבד**. ועת שאבדם בגולה, שנאמר (ויקרא כו:לח) ואבדתם בגוים: **עת לשמור** — (במדבר ו:כד) יברכך ה׳ וישמרך, כשאתם עושים רצונו; **ועת להשליך** — (דברים כט:כז) וישלכם אל־ארץ אחרת: **(ז) עת לקרוע** מלכות בית דוד (מלכים א׳ יד:ח) ואקרע את־הממלכה וגומר; **ועת לתפור** — (יחזקאל לז:יז) והיו לאחדים בידך, (שם:כב) ולא יחצו עוד לשתי ממלכות: **עת לחשות**. פעמים שאדם שותק ומקבל שכר, שנאמר (ויקרא י:ג) וידם אהרן, וזכה שנתייחד הדבור עמו, שנאמר (שם י:ח־ט) וידבר ה׳ אל אהרן... יין ושכר אל־תשת; **ועת לדבר** — (שמות טו:א) אז ישיר־משה, (שופטים ה:א) ותשר דבורה, (הושע יד:ג) קחו עמכם דברים: **(ח) עת לאהב**. שנאמר (ואהבך) [(מלאכי א:ב) אהבתי אתכם]; **ועת לשנא**. שנאמר (כל רעתם בגלגל) [(ירמיה יב:ח) נתנה עלי בקולה] על־כן שנאתיה: **(ט) מה־יתרון העושה**. מה יתרון של עושה רע בכל שהוא עמל? גם הוא עתו יבא — והכל אבד.

6] A TIME TO SEEK AND A TIME TO FORSAKE . . . Especially painful is the need sometimes to make a definite choice between one alternative and the other.

7] A TIME TO KEEP SILENCE . . . In emotional situations, one suffers because of the necessity to exercise restraint and remain silent for fear of aggravating the situation — another evil that visits both rich and poor.

5] There is a time to cast away stones and a time to gather stones together; a time to embrace and a time to refrain from embracing.

6] There is a time to seek and a time to forsake; a time to keep and a time to discard.

7] There is a time to rend and a time to sew; a time to keep silence and a time to speak up.

8] There is a time to love and a time to hate; a time for war and a time for peace.

9] What profit has the worker in his labor?

8] A TIME TO LOVE AND A TIME TO HATE. Everyone experiences pleasant situations that call forth love and admiration; everyone experiences circumstances which arouse feelings of hatred.

A TIME FOR WAR AND A TIME FOR PEACE. War and peace provide ample opportunity for expressions of love and hatred. Koheleth may be alluding here to the fact that good and evil befall nations even as they do individuals.

9] WHAT PROFIT . . . There is no profit. There is nothing man can do to escape evil. All the wealth a man can accumulate as a result of his labor will not help him live the completely pleasant life. One cannot run away from evil. The many forms of evil and its ubiquity leave no room or place for escape.

Too often, evil is generated by man himself, by his philosophy of life, by his attitude towards higher values. The evil may come from within rather than from without. Whatever the source of evil, the accumulation of wealth will not protect one from the effects of evil.

י] רָאִיתִי אֶת־הָעִנְיָן אֲשֶׁר נָתַן אֱלֹהִים לִבְנֵי הָאָדָם לַעֲנוֹת בּוֹ:
יא] אֶת־הַכֹּל עָשָׂה יָפֶה בְעִתּוֹ גַּם אֶת־הָעֹלָם נָתַן בְּלִבָּם מִבְּלִי
אֲשֶׁר לֹא־יִמְצָא הָאָדָם אֶת־הַמַּעֲשֶׂה אֲשֶׁר־עָשָׂה הָאֱלֹהִים
מֵרֹאשׁ וְעַד־סוֹף:

(י) **העניין.** המנהג: **לענות.** להתנהג: (יא) **יפה בעתו.** בעת הטובה יפה היא לבא תשלום שכר מעשה הטוב, ובעת הרעה ראויה היא לתשלום מעשה הרע: **גם את־העלם נתן בלבם וגו׳.** גם את חכמת העולם אשר נתן בלב הבריות לא נתן הכל בלב כל אחד ואחד, אלא זה קצת וזה קצת, כדי שלא ימצא האדם את כל מעשה הקדוש ברוך הוא לדעת אותו ולא ידע את עת פקודתו ובמה יכשל, כדי שיתן לב לשוב שידאג ויאמר היום או מחר אמות; ולכך כתוב כאן העלם חסר — לשון העלמה (תנחומא קדושים ח), שאם ידע האדם יום מיתתו קרובה, לא יבנה בית ולא יטע כרם; לכך הוא אומר שהכל עשה יפה בעתו, זה שיש עת למיתה — דבר יפה הוא, שסומך האדם לומר שמא עדיין עת מיתתי רחוקה,

10–15 / The need for evil and the antidote of evil

10] THE MATTER . . . BECAME CLEAR TO ME. The matter of evil. Why should there be evil? Why does Elohim allow persons to suffer — all persons?

Koheleth repeats what he has stated in verse 1:13 in regard to Elohim. Man is entitled to reward only if he has freedom of choice. There could not be any freedom of choice if the righteous enjoyed only good and suffered no evil, while the wicked suffered evil and enjoyed no good. For under such circumstances, only a crass fool could choose evil. But Elohim is determined to reward man; therefore He must give man the opportunity to serve Him as a matter of choice. When man serves Elohim in spite of his affliction, when man serves Elohim in spite of the fact that he sees many a wicked person enjoying good, then he is entitled to reward. This is so if we understand evil to mean pain and frustration.

10] The matter which Elohim has given man to be afflicted with, became clear to me.

11] He has made everything properly, to function in its due time; He has placed a sense of eternity in man's heart; except that man cannot discover Elohim's plan of history from beginning to end.

However, evil has another sense — punishment. In this sense, affliction is necessary to remind man that he must improve his ways. Each instance of suffering is a message of warning and a call for reflection and repentance. In this sense, the punishment is not an unmixed evil, but is also good.

11] PROPERLY TO FUNCTION IN ITS DUE TIME . . . Elohim has created good and evil and has appointed them to visit man each in its due time according to His plan and the merits of the individual.

A SENSE OF ETERNITY IN MAN'S HEART . . . Besides giving man freedom of choice, Elohim has raised man above the level of the animal by planting in him a sense of eternity. This spiritual power is granted to man so that he may more readily rise above evil and recognize the existence of Elohim, Who created the universe and to Whom man is accountable.

The sense of eternity manifests itself in man's awe when he is exposed to lofty mountains, wide spaces and sky; in man's inspiration when he sees a beautiful landscape; in man's being carried away by spellbinding music or the song of birds; in short, in man's ability to lose himself in breathtaking natural phenomena.

MAN CANNOT DISCOVER . . . In spite of man's sense of eternity, he is incapable of understanding the complexities of good and

יב) יָדַעְתִּי כִּי אֵין טוֹב בָּם כִּי אִם־לִשְׂמוֹחַ וְלַעֲשׂוֹת טוֹב בְּחַיָּיו׃
יג) וְגַם כָּל־הָאָדָם שֶׁיֹּאכַל וְשָׁתָה וְרָאָה טוֹב בְּכָל־עֲמָלוֹ מַתַּת
אֱלֹהִים הִיא׃
יד) יָדַעְתִּי כִּי כָּל־אֲשֶׁר יַעֲשֶׂה הָאֱלֹהִים הוּא יִהְיֶה לְעוֹלָם עָלָיו
אֵין לְהוֹסִיף וּמִמֶּנּוּ אֵין לִגְרֹעַ וְהָאֱלֹהִים עָשָׂה שֶׁיִּרְאוּ מִלְּפָנָיו׃

ובונה בית ונוטע כרם, וזו יפה שנעלם מן הבריות: **(יב) ידעתי עתה,** הואיל ונעלם עת הפקודה, **כי אין טוב** בבריות **כי אם־לשמוח** בחלקו **ולעשות הטוב** בעיני בוראו בעוד שהוא חי: **(יג) וראה טוב.** תורה ומצוות: **(יד) ידעתי כי כל־אשר יעשה** הקדוש ברוך הוא במעשה בראשית הוא ראוי להיות לעולם ואין לשנותו לא בתוספת ולא בגרוע, וכשנשתנה — האלהים ציוה ועשה שישתנה, כדי **שיראו מלפניו:** אוקיינוס פרץ גבולו בדור אנוש והציף שלישו של

evil and the historical considerations of Elohim in meting out reward and punishment to nations and individuals.

12] FROM AMONG THE CHOICES . . . There is only one antidote to evil — to accept it gracefully. Man is witness to evil in the form of pain and suffering, in the inequities among men, in the tragedies of history, and in natural catastrophes. There is no way of avoiding evil. However, evil must not be permitted to lead to despondency.

THAN TO BE HAPPY . . . Man can face the challenges of this world only if he maintains a happy frame of mind. He must be armed with a basic optimism which enables him to overcome his frustrations with a smile. To despair is to be defeated before one has started. Optimism and a happy frame of mind are the foundation elements of active productivity and joyful living.

AND TO PERFORM GOOD DEEDS . . . In chapters 1 and 2, Koheleth taught us that selfish joys and pleasures do not bring

12] I know that there is nothing better, from among the choices, than for man to be happy and to perform good deeds during his lifetime.

13] Indeed, when a man eats and drinks and sees only good in all his labor, that is the gift of Elohim.

14] I know that whatever Elohim does will always

lasting happiness in their wake. But if man makes the performance of good deeds for others part of his daily living, he is sure to find happiness as a by-product of his efforts. Only when man expends himself for causes greater than himself does man enjoy his own living.

13] WHEN A MAN EATS AND DRINKS ... A restatement of the vital principle mentioned above (2:24). Elohim wants man to partake of the good of this world. Man should eat and drink and enjoy whatever he possesses, be it abundant or meager.

AND SEES ONLY GOOD ... To see only good, that is the key thought — in spite of all frustration and suffering to see only good. That is the only way to overcome evil.

THAT IS THE GIFT OF ELOHIM ... In the earlier statement (2:24), "from the hand of Elohim." Koheleth is convinced that man shows his affinity to Elohim when he "sees only good." The fact that man rises above his suffering and maintains optimism, despite the evil that befalls him, is an indication that he sees the hand of Elohim behind all phenomena and occurrences.

טו) מַה־שֶּׁהָיָה כְּבָר הוּא וַאֲשֶׁר לִהְיוֹת כְּבָר הָיָה וְהָאֱלֹהִים יְבַקֵּשׁ אֶת־נִרְדָּף:

עולם, והאלהים עשה שייראו מלפניו; שבעת ימים נשתנה הלוך החמה בדור המבול לזרוח במערב ולשקוע במזרח, כדי שייראו מלפניו; חמה חזרה לאחוריה עשר מעלות בימי חזקיהו, ובימי אחז אביו נתקצר היום ונתרבה הלילה ביום מותו כדי שלא יהא נספד — כל זה כדי שייראו מלפניו; לפיכך אין טוב לאדם לעסוק אלא במצוותיו ולירא מלפניו: (טו) **מה שהיה כבר הוא.** **מה שהיה** מלפנינו — **כבר הוא** עשוי, וראינוהו או שמענוהו מאחרים שראוהו; ויש לנו להעיד עליו שראינו שהקדוש ברוך הוא מבקש את הנרדפים: יעקב נרדף, עשו רודף — (מלאכי א: ב־ג) ואהב את־יעקב ואת־עשו שנאתי; מצרים רודפים את ישראל — מצרים טבעו בים וישראל הלכו ביד רמה: **ואשר עתיד להיות** עוד באחרונה הוא דוגמת מה שכבר היה, כאשר בראשונה כן באחרונה; אין הקדוש ברוך הוא משנה מדותיו בעולם (ע׳ קה״ר): **והאלהים יבקש את־נרדף.** ליפרע מן הרודף; לפיכך מה יתרונו של עושה הרעה באשר הוא עמל, הרי סופו להשתלם:

14] ONE CANNOT ADD TO IT NOR SUBTRACT FROM IT . . . Here Koheleth alludes to the commonly expressed wish: would that there were more good in the world and less evil. But Elohim knows better how much good and evil is needed in this world and He has apportioned them accordingly.

SO THAT MAN WILL FEAR HIM. In spite of man's claim that he can build the good society on "reason and love," the facts are that where there is no fear of Elohim, the law of the jungle prevails, as Koheleth will soon point out (v. 16–22).

15] WHAT HAPPENED IN THE PAST, EXISTS TODAY . . . Koheleth alludes to another argument: perhaps primitive man

be so; one cannot add to it nor subtract from it. Elohim has done this so that man will fear Him.

15] What happened in the past, exists today; and what will be, existed in the past; Elohim seeks the pursued man.

needed punishment and control by fear, but modern man is different: it is time to abandon all evil. The answer is that modern man is no different from the first man.

No sooner is man freed from labor, anxiety, and troubles than he forgets his moral responsibilities and follows his emotions and passions. "What happened in the past exists today."

ELOHIM SEEKS THE PURSUED MAN. For man's own good, Elohim gives man the feeling that he is pursued by troubles and worries, for only then does he turn to Elohim for help. The man who senses that he can earn his bread with ease is likely to say, "My strength and my power have procured me this wealth" (Deuteronomy 8:17). He is not likely to recognize Elohim.

But Elohim seeks man's affinity. He wants to help man and wants man to appeal to Him for help. He wants to keep His ties with man. *He wants man to be pursued because He seeks the pursued man.*

טז] וְעוֹד רָאִיתִי תַּחַת הַשָּׁמֶשׁ מְקוֹם הַמִּשְׁפָּט שָׁמָּה הָרֶשַׁע וּמְקוֹם
הַצֶּדֶק שָׁמָּה הָרָשַׁע׃
יז] אָמַרְתִּי אֲנִי בְּלִבִּי אֶת־הַצַּדִּיק וְאֶת־הָרָשָׁע יִשְׁפֹּט הָאֱלֹהִים
כִּי־עֵת לְכָל־חֵפֶץ וְעַל כָּל־הַמַּעֲשֶׂה שָׁם׃

(טז) **מקום המשפט וגו׳.** ראיתי ברוח הקודש מקום לשכת הגזית בירושלים, שהיתה (ישעיה א:כא) מלאתי משפט — **שמה** ישפטו רשע, כמו שנאמר (מיכה ג:יא) ראשיה בשחד ישפטו, וראיתי פורענותם; **ומקום הצדק.** שער התווך, שהיה מקום חתוך הלכות (סנהדרין קג ע״א) — **שמה הרשע,** שם ישבו שרסכים רב־סריס נרגל שראצר רב־מג (ירמיה לט:ג) ונבוכדנצר וחילותיו, ודנין את ישראל בייסורים קשים ומשפטי מות (ויקרא רבה פרשה ד, וע׳ קה״ר): **שמה הרשע.** טעמו למעלה, לומר שהוא שם דבר כמו הרשע, [והיה ראוי לינקד בסגול הרי״ש] אלא לפי שהוא סוף פסוק נהפך לינקד קמץ גדול, ואף על פי שבכל מקום לא מצינו לו עוד שמתהפך באתנחתא וסוף פסוק:
(יז) **אמרתי אני בלבי וגו׳.** לפיכך אני אומר את הכל שופט הקדוש ברוך הוא לאחר זמן, ואף על פי שמתעכב הדבר סופו לבא אל שעתו, כי שעה יש לכל חפץ, אף לפורענות, ולפקודת הדין יש עת מתי יבא: **ועל כל־המעשה** שעשה האדם שם ישפטוהו בבא עת הפקודה; **שם** — באותו העת ניתן זמן לכל המעשה להשפט עליו, (אבי) [אבבא] חוטרי מילי ואבי דרי חושבנא (שבת לב ע״א):

16–22 / Can man build a just society on his own?

16] Again, I observed, under the sun . . . After having enlightened us on some of the ways of Elohim and man's proper reaction thereto, Koheleth returns to another critical evaluation of the "under-the-sun" philosophy. The adherents of this philosophy are frequently heard to express the opinion that man, on his own, is able to build the good society on the basis of reason and love. To this Koheleth takes exception.

in the place of justice . . . wickedness. Since the "under-the-sun" philosophy finds no place for Elohim in the universe, the fear of Heaven does not serve to restrain materialistic

16] Again, I observed, under the sun, that in the place of justice there was wickedness, and in the place of righteousness there was wickedness.

17] I said to myself, both the righteous and wicked Elohim will judge, for there is a time for every desire and every deed — there.

man from doing evil. The only deterrent would be man's intelligence and his reasonable expectation that human understanding would prevent one man from exploiting the other; it would logically be of mutual advantage for man and his neighbor to cooperate with each other.

Unfortunately, says Koheleth, logic is not enough. For history has shown that even in the place of justice one finds wickedness, even in the place of righteousness. Even those people appointed by man to enforce the human legal code are themselves tainted with wickedness. Where there is no fear of Elohim, there is surely no fear of man.

17] I SAID TO MYSELF . . . A parenthetical statement. Of course, I, Koheleth, as a man of faith, am certain that such wickedness and hypocrisy will not go unpunished.

BOTH THE RIGHTEOUS AND THE WICKED . . . Perhaps Koheleth has in mind here one and the same individual who pretends to be righteous but is actually wicked, who pretends to minister justly but accepts bribes and favors. It is inevitable that he will be judged by Elohim.

A TIME FOR EVERY DESIRE . . . Man is brought to judgment not only for his deeds but also for harboring evil desires. Man is controlled more by his desires and his will than by his reason. The initial evil thought is pardonable as accidental.

יח] אָמַרְתִּי אֲנִי בְּלִבִּי עַל־דִּבְרַת בְּנֵי הָאָדָם לְבָרָם הָאֱלֹהִים
וְלִרְאוֹת שְׁהֶם־בְּהֵמָה הֵמָּה לָהֶם׃
יט] כִּי מִקְרֶה בְנֵי־הָאָדָם וּמִקְרֶה הַבְּהֵמָה וּמִקְרֶה אֶחָד לָהֶם
כְּמוֹת זֶה כֵּן מוֹת זֶה וְרוּחַ אֶחָד לַכֹּל וּמוֹתַר הָאָדָם מִן־
הַבְּהֵמָה אָיִן כִּי הַכֹּל הָבֶל׃
כ] הַכֹּל הוֹלֵךְ אֶל־מָקוֹם אֶחָד הַכֹּל הָיָה מִן־הֶעָפָר וְהַכֹּל שָׁב
אֶל־הֶעָפָר׃

(יח) **אמרתי אני בלבי**, בראותי זאת, **על־דברת בני האדם**, שאחזו להם מדת גאות לנהוג שררה ורבנות בקטנים מהם, **לברם** הקדוש ברוך הוא, **להודיעם** שאין שררתם כלום, **ולהראותם שהם** ואף השרים והמלכים **בהמה המה להם**, כשאר בהמה וחיה המה לעצמם: (יט) **כי מקרה בני־האדם וגו׳**. הוא טעם הדבר אשר נתן מקרה ופגע לבני אדם, ויש מקרה ופגע לבהמה — **ומקרה אחד** לשניהם נתן, כי כשם שזה מת כך זה מת, **ומותר האדם מן־הבהמה אין**. ויתרונו והצלחתו של אדם יותר מן הבהמה אינו נראה משמת, **כי הכל** נהפך להיות **הבל**

But the fostering of an evil thought, allowing it to incubate to the point where it can lead to actual implementation, is as improper as the performance of the deed.

THERE. In the world to come, at the bar of heavenly justice, there will be accounting for every deed and for every desire incubated and fostered.

18] IN REGARD TO WHAT MEN SAY. This refers to verses 19–21.

ELOHIM HAS TESTED THEM . . . Elohim gave man freedom of choice; He patiently waited to see whether the man of the "under-the-sun" philosophy would find a way to a truly civilized society. He waited to see whether people would abide by man-made laws arrived at democratically. He waited to see whether people and nations would respect each other's fundamental rights. He waited to see whether man would

18] I thought to myself, in regard to what men say: Elohim has tested them and revealed to them that they are like beasts to each other.

19] [They say,] "The fate of men and the fate of beasts is the same; as one dies so does the other — there is one spirit in all; the advantage of man over beast is naught, all is vanity.

20] "All go to one place; all come from dust and all return to dust.

improve not only the physical conditions of living but also the moral and social relationships between man and man.

REVEALED . . . THAT THEY ARE LIKE BEASTS . . . But as history unfolded itself, it was revealed that men cannot control their animal instincts by man-made laws and understandings. It was revealed to all that selfish and prejudiced motives were behind the beastly actions of men and that these motives were more powerful than any man-made regulations.

From the "under-the-sun" point of view there is practically no significant difference between man and beast. As expressed in the next three verses (19–21), this philosophy holds: there is no advantage of man over beast; all go to one place and there is no higher spirit in man. Such a philosophy must ultimately lead to the degradation of the dignity of man, to beastly behavior.

19] FATE OF MEN AND . . . BEASTS IS THE SAME. If man is looked upon as just a more highly developed animal, then ultimately the law of the jungle will prevail among men as it does among animals.

20] ALL GO TO ONE PLACE . . . Then why try to live on a higher level than the beast?

כא) מִי יוֹדֵעַ רוּחַ בְּנֵי הָאָדָם הָעֹלָה הִיא לְמָעְלָה וְרוּחַ הַבְּהֵמָה
הַיֹּרֶדֶת הִיא לְמַטָּה לָאָרֶץ׃
כב) וְרָאִיתִי כִּי אֵין טוֹב מֵאֲשֶׁר יִשְׂמַח הָאָדָם בְּמַעֲשָׂיו כִּי־הוּא
חֶלְקוֹ כִּי מִי יְבִיאֶנּוּ לִרְאוֹת בְּמֶה שֶׁיִּהְיֶה אַחֲרָיו׃

לשוב אל העפר: **(כא) מי יודע.** (יואל ב:יד) מי יודע ישוב; מי הוא אשר מבין ונותן לב, שרוח בני האדם היא העלה למעלה ועומדת בדין, ורוח הבהמה היא הירדת למטה לארץ ואין לה ליתן דין וחשבון, וצריך שלא להתנהג כבהמה שאינה מקפדת על מעשיה: **(כב) וראיתי** בכל אלה **כי אין טוב** לאדם **מאשר ישמח האדם במעשיו** — ביגיע כפיו ישמח ויאכל, ולא להרחיב כשאול נפשו לחמוד להתעשר להרבות לא לו, **כי־הוא חלקו** — יגיע כפיו הוא החלק הניתן לו משמים ובו ישמח, **כי מי יביאנו לראות** לאחר שמת **במה שיהיה** לבניו, אם יצליחו גם הם בעושר שאסף הוא והניח להם או לא יצליחו:

21] WHO KNOWS . . . A cynical question. In other words, there is no higher spirit in man. If there is no Elohim, then there cannot be any man in the image of Elohim.

22] I PERCEIVED . . . Man-made societies will not bring about the good life and ultimate happiness. Man cannot do away with evil. There is only one road to happiness and one antidote to evil.

TO REJOICE IN HIS WORKS . . . HIS PORTION . . . Only when man is content with what he has can he be happy. Only when man accepts evil gracefully can he be free of the chains of despair. Man was made to partake in the good of this

21] "Who knows whether the spirit of man rises upward or whether the spirit of the beast descends down to earth?"

22] I perceived that there is nothing better for man than to rejoice in his works, for that is his portion; for who will bring him to see what will be afterwards?

world; to eat, drink and be merry; to count his blessings and to recognize them as the gifts of Elohim, in spite of any evil he may suffer.

TO SEE WHAT WILL BE AFTERWARDS. It is wrong to ask man to deny himself the good of this world and to look forward to happiness only in the world to come. It is demanding too much of man to look forward only to a good that he has never seen. Elohim has given man a basically complete world, supplied with all that is needed to enjoy living in that world. Elohim wants man to enjoy life, live in contentment and serve Elohim in optimism; not to withdraw from the world and society — not even in order to enjoy another world afterwards.

Chapter 4

COOPERATION

The load which a person can lift up
by himself is only one third
of the weight he can carry
if people assist him in lifting it up.

Talmud

פ ר ק ר ב י ע י

א] וְשַׁבְתִּי אֲנִי וָאֶרְאֶה אֶת־כָּל־הָעֲשֻׁקִים אֲשֶׁר נַעֲשִׂים תַּחַת
הַשָּׁמֶשׁ וְהִנֵּה דִּמְעַת הָעֲשֻׁקִים וְאֵין לָהֶם מְנַחֵם וּמִיַּד עֹשְׁקֵיהֶם
כֹּחַ וְאֵין לָהֶם מְנַחֵם:
ב] וְשַׁבֵּחַ אֲנִי אֶת־הַמֵּתִים שֶׁכְּבָר מֵתוּ מִן־הַחַיִּים אֲשֶׁר הֵמָּה
חַיִּים עֲדֶנָה:
ג] וְטוֹב מִשְּׁנֵיהֶם אֵת אֲשֶׁר־עֲדֶן לֹא הָיָה אֲשֶׁר לֹא־רָאָה אֶת־
הַמַּעֲשֶׂה הָרָע אֲשֶׁר נַעֲשָׂה תַּחַת הַשָּׁמֶשׁ:

(א) **ושבתי אני ואראה** ברוח הקודש **את־כל־העשקים**, הנעשים עשוקים בגיהנם במעשים **אשר נעשים תחת השמש** — תחת חליפיה של התורה: **והנה דמעת העשקים.** בוכים על נפשותם העשוקות ביד מלאכי משחית ואכזרים, וכן הוא אומר (תהלים פד: ז) עברי בעמק הבכא מעין ישיתוהו — אלו יורדי גיהנם (עירובין יט ע״א), ואף מקרא זה כך נדרש בספרי (ע׳ דברים יא: כו): **ומיד עשקיהם כח.** עושקיהם מכריחים ותוקפים אותם בכח: (ב) **שכבר מתו.** עד שלא שלט בהם יצר הרע הזה לדחותם מן הקדוש ברוך הוא, כגון אבות הראשונים שלא נענה משה אלא על ידיהם, וכגון דוד אבי שלא נעניתי אני בעשרים וארבע רננות עד שאמרתי (דברי הימים ב׳ ו: מב) זכרה לחסדי דויד עבדך (שבת ל ע״א): (ג) **עדן.** עדיין: **אשר לא־ראה את־המעשה.** ראיתי במדרש קהלת (קה״ר; וע׳ חגיגה יג ע״א ורש״י שם) אלו תשע מאות ושבעים וארבע דורות, שקומטו להיבראות ולא נבראו:

1–3 / Oppression is characteristic of man-made societies

1] ALL THE ACTS OF OPPRESSION . . . After a pause, in which Koheleth reminds us of his solution to the problem of happiness, he returns to the theme begun in verse 3:18: man on his own cannot bring about the just society. Men behave toward each other like beasts; the mighty oppress the weak; the larger nations subdue the smaller nations.

COMMITTED UNDER THE SUN . . . The "under-the-sun" philosophy does not see man in the image of God, does not respect

CHAPTER FOUR

1] I returned and observed all the acts of oppression that are committed under the sun. Here
are the tears of the oppressed with no one to
comfort them; and power comes forth from the
hands of their oppressors; but there is no one
to comfort them.

2] And so, I praise the dead who have already died,
over and above the living who are still alive.

3] And better than both of these is he who has
not yet been born and therefore has not seen the
evil that is performed under the sun.

man any more than the animal. It respects only strength and success, a reflection of what it believes it sees in nature: a struggle for existence and survival of the fittest.

AND POWER COMES FORTH ... The mighty grow mightier and the weak grow weaker and no one comes forth to champion the rights of the weaker. The law of the jungle prevails.

2] OVER AND ABOVE THE LIVING ... In a world where man does not respect his fellow man, life is laden with fear, distrust, worry and anxiety. Therefore, one can have praise only for the dead who have finally escaped this agony.

3] AND BETTER THAN BOTH OF THESE ... The living continue to struggle in a dreadful world; the dead have had their full share. Only he who was not yet born is spared all the evil.

EVIL THAT IS PERFORMED UNDER THE SUN. "Under the sun" there is no foundation of faith on which to build a super-

ד] וְרָאִיתִי אֲנִי אֶת־כָּל־עָמָל וְאֵת כָּל־כִּשְׁרוֹן הַמַּעֲשֶׂה כִּי הִיא
קִנְאַת־אִישׁ מֵרֵעֵהוּ גַּם־זֶה הֶבֶל וּרְעוּת רוּחַ:
ה] הַכְּסִיל חֹבֵק אֶת־יָדָיו וְאֹכֵל אֶת־בְּשָׂרוֹ:
ו] טוֹב מְלֹא כַף נָחַת מִמְּלֹא חָפְנַיִם עָמָל וּרְעוּת רוּחַ:
ז] וְשַׁבְתִּי אֲנִי וָאֶרְאֶה הֶבֶל תַּחַת הַשָּׁמֶשׁ:
ח] יֵשׁ אֶחָד וְאֵין שֵׁנִי גַּם בֵּן וָאָח אֵין־לוֹ וְאֵין קֵץ לְכָל־עֲמָלוֹ

(ד) **וראיתי אני את־כל־עמל.** הן העבירות שהן עמל בעיני הקדוש ברוך הוא: **ואת כל־כשרון המעשה** שאינו לשם שמים אלא **לקנאת איש מרעהו,** ששניהם הבל: **כי היא קנאת־איש.** אשר היא קנאת איש מרעהו: (ה) **הכסיל** — הרשע, **חבק את־ידיו** ואינו יגע ואינו אוכל אלא מן הגזל, **ואכל את־בשרו** ליום הדין, שרואה צדיקים בכבוד והוא נידון; כך נדרש בספרי (שם): (ו) **טוב מלא כף נחת.** להיות קונה נכסים מעט ומיגיעו, שיהא בהן נחת רוח ליוצרו, **ממלא חפנים.** נכסים הרבה בעבירה, שהוא עמל ועצבות רוח לפני המקום: (ז) **תחת השמש.** כמו תחת השמים: (ח) **יש אחד ואין שני.** יש לך אדם שעושה דבריו ביחידי: **גם בן ואח אין־לו.** אם תלמיד חכם הוא, אינו קונה לו תלמיד שהוא כבן ולא

structure of optimism; there is no all-out desire to comfort the weak and poor; there is no purpose for living other than self-aggrandizement; there is only a constant rat-race for material gain.

4-8 / Labor and contentment are necessary for the happy life

4) THE OUTCOME OF MAN'S ENVY OF HIS NEIGHBOR . . . In this verse and the next, Koheleth describes two extremes in a materialistic society: the ambitious man and the slothful individual. For either one, life is devoid of meaning.

The ambitious man is engulfed in an endless pursuit of money and possessions. Envy of his neighbor is the driving force of his highly geared activity. It spurs him on to super-

4] And I observed that all hard labor and striving for excellence in performance is the outcome of man's envy of his neighbor. This, too, is vanity and chasing after wind.

5] The fool folds his hands together and consequently has naught to eat but his own flesh.

6] Better one handful earned in contentment than two handfuls earned in vexing labor and chasing after wind.

7] I returned and observed another form of vanity under the sun.

8] There is a lonely individual with none other beside him; he has neither son nor brother. Yet there is no end to his labor and his eye is never

sede his neighbor, and then his neighbor's neighbor, *ad infinitum*. He is engaged in a vain chasing after wind.

5] THE FOOL FOLDS HIS HANDS . . . On the other extreme, we have the fool who dreads the competition and therefore does nothing. He too, suffers, for he has naught to eat but his own flesh.

6] BETTER . . . CONTENTMENT . . . Alas, sighs Koheleth, if these people knew the joy of labor and contentment, how much happier would they be. If earning two handfuls requires vexing labor and chasing after wind, how much sweeter is one handful in contentment.

8] THERE IS A LONELY INDIVIDUAL . . . Koheleth describes here the extremes to which the materialistic drive for money

גַּם־עינו [עֵינוֹ] לֹא־תִשְׂבַּע עֹשֶׁר וּלְמִי אֲנִי עָמֵל וּמְחַסֵּר
אֶת־נַפְשִׁי מִטּוֹבָה גַּם־זֶה הֶבֶל וְעִנְיַן רָע הוּא:

חבר שהוא כאח; ואם רווק הוא, אינו נושא אשה להיות לו כאח לעזר ולהוליד בן; ואם סוחר הוא, אינו קונה לו שותפים ויצא לדרך יחידי: ואין קץ לכל־עמלו. יגע בגירסא; ואם סוחר הוא, עמל בפרקמטיא: גם־עינו לא־תשבע עושר. לא יהא שבע בטעמי תורה, שהרבה תורה לומד אדם מתלמידיו; ולענין הממון — רודף תמיד אחר הממון: ולמי אני עמל. מאחר שאיני מעמיד תלמידים ואיני נושא אשה להוליד בנים:

may lead. Even if we could find some defense for the family man to work day and night in order to support his dependents, it is extremely difficult to excuse the lonely miser who accumulates wealth over and above his needs and still continues to slave and deprive himself of pleasure.

satisfied with his wealth. He never pauses to ask, "For whom do I labor and deprive myself of pleasure?" This, too, is vanity and a grievous matter.

NO END TO HIS LABOR . . . If one has no higher purpose in life, then the means become an end and all his efforts are directed toward the accumulation of wealth.

HIS EYE IS NEVER SATISFIED . . . Jealousy knows no end and envy no limit. In the words of the Rabbis: "He who has one hundred wants two." Koheleth, in the next chapter (5:9), says: "He who loves money will never have enough money."

ט] טוֹבִים הַשְּׁנַיִם מִן־הָאֶחָד אֲשֶׁר יֵשׁ־לָהֶם שָׂכָר טוֹב בַּעֲמָלָם׃
י] כִּי אִם־יִפֹּלוּ הָאֶחָד יָקִים אֶת־חֲבֵרוֹ וְאִילוֹ הָאֶחָד שֶׁיִּפּוֹל
וְאֵין שֵׁנִי לַהֲקִימוֹ׃
יא] גַּם אִם־יִשְׁכְּבוּ שְׁנַיִם וְחַם לָהֶם וּלְאֶחָד אֵיךְ יֵחָם׃
יב] וְאִם־יִתְקְפוֹ הָאֶחָד הַשְּׁנַיִם יַעַמְדוּ נֶגְדּוֹ וְהַחוּט הַמְשֻׁלָּשׁ לֹא
בִמְהֵרָה יִנָּתֵק׃

(ט) **טובים השנים** לכל דבר **מן־האחד**; לפיכך יקנה לו אדם חבר וישא אשה, **אשר יש־להם** יותר ריוח **בעמלם**; הרבה מלאכה נעשית בשנים, שאין היחיד מתחיל בה לבדו, (י) **כי אם־יפלו**. כמשמעו. ולענין המשנה — אם תקפה עליו משנה שלו חבירו מחזירה לו, או אם יכשל ולא דקדק את אשר שמע מפי רבו בא חבירו ומעמידו על האמת (מגילה ה ע״ב, קה״ר); **ואילו**. ואוי לו: (יא) **וחם להם**. כמשמעו. ולענין זכר ונקבה — מתחממים זה מזה ומולידים: (יב) **ואם־יתקפו האחד**. אם באו לסטים עליו לתקפו, אם שנים הם — **יעמדו נגדו**, וכל שכן אם שלשה הם — **החוט המשלש לא במהרה ינתק** (מדרש תהלים נט: א). דבר אחר, מי שהוא תלמיד חכם ובנו ובן בנו, שוב אין תורה פוסקת מזרעו, שנאמר (ישעיה נט: כא) לא־ימושו מפיך ומפי זרעך ומפי זרע זרעך (בבא מציעא פה ע״א). דבר אחר, **חוט המשולש** — [כל שישנו] במקרא ובמשנה ובדרך ארץ, **לא במהרה** הוא חוטא (קדושין מ ע״ב). בפנים אחרים נדרש במדרש (ע׳ קה״ר, לעיל פס׳ ח) **יש אחד ואין שני** לו; אבל אין סדר כל המקראות הללו מתיישב עליהם:

9–12 / The advantage of companionship

9] Two are better than one . . . Turning form the dismal figure of the lonely miser, Koheleth praises the altruism of cooperation and companionship. People should respect each other, should work together, and should assist each other.

9] Two are better than one, since they have a good reward for their labor.

10] If they fall, each can help the other to rise; but woe to him who is alone when he falls and there is no one to lift him up.

11] Again, if two lie together, they can be warm; but how can one be warm alone?

12] And if an individual attacks, both can stand up to him; however, a threefold cord is better still, for it cannot be quickly severed.

SINCE THEY HAVE GOOD REWARD . . . The companionship itself is good reward even if there should be no material gain. Rashi says companionship refers here to a friend or to a wife. Man should not face the trials of life alone.

10] IF THEY FALL . . . A true friend is one who not only shares in joy but is also present in time of trouble — who is ready to help when things are not going well.

12] AND IF AN INDIVIDUAL ATTACKS . . . No matter what danger threatens, be it physical or mental, two can stand up to it better than one.

A THREEFOLD CORD . . . If two friends working together have so many advantages, how much greater is the advantage when three or more form a solid friendship.

יג] טוֹב יֶלֶד מִסְכֵּן וְחָכָם מִמֶּלֶךְ זָקֵן וּכְסִיל אֲשֶׁר לֹא־יָדַע
לְהִזָּהֵר עוֹד׃
יד] כִּי־מִבֵּית הָסוּרִים יָצָא לִמְלֹךְ כִּי גַּם בְּמַלְכוּתוֹ נוֹלַד רָשׁ׃
טו] רָאִיתִי אֶת־כָּל־הַחַיִּים הַמְהַלְּכִים תַּחַת הַשָּׁמֶשׁ עִם הַיֶּלֶד
הַשֵּׁנִי אֲשֶׁר יַעֲמֹד תַּחְתָּיו׃
טז] אֵין־קֵץ לְכָל־הָעָם לְכֹל אֲשֶׁר־הָיָה לִפְנֵיהֶם גַּם הָאַחֲרוֹנִים

(יג) **טוב ילד מסכן וחכם.** זה יצר טוב, ולמה נקרא ילד? שאינו בא באדם עד י״ג שנה: **מסכן.** שאין האיברים שומעים לו כמו ליצר הרע: **וחכם.** שמשכיל את האדם לדרך טובה: **ממלך זקן וכסיל.** יצר הרע, שהוא שליט על כל האיברים: **זקן.** שמשעה שנולד הוולד הוא נתון בו, שנאמר (בראשית ד:ז) לפתח חטאת רבץ: **וכסיל.** שמתעהו בדרך רעה — כך נדרש במדרש (ע׳ מדרש תהלים ט:ב): **אשר לא־ידע להזהר עוד.** שהרי הזקין ואינו מקבל תוכחה: (יד) **כי־מבית הסורים יצא למלך.** ממקום הטנופת וסרחון, כדמתרגמינן (שמות ז:כא) ויבאש — וסרי: **כי גם במלכותו,** משמלך באדם, **נולד רש.** המסכן, הטוב ממנו ובא מתוך טהרה, ולא מתוך טנופת הרחם — כך דרשוהו במדרש (עי״ש; וע׳ קה״ר). דבר אחר, **כי טוב ילד מסכן** וגומר. כמשמעו. **אשר לא־ידע להזהר עוד.** שכבר הזקין ברשעו וכסילותו: **כי־מבית הסורים יצא למלך.** כי הילד המסכן, סופו שיאמרו עליו שיצא למלוך מתוך עוניו ומבית אסוריו [שהרי סמ״ך של הסורים נקוד רפי והרי הוא כמו האסורים], שכן מצינו ביוסף שמלך מתוך יציאת בית האסורים (בראשית רבה פט ג, וע׳ קה״ר), וכן דוד (שמואל ב, ז:ח) אני לקחתיך מן־הנוה מאחר הצאן: **כי גם במלכותו נולד רש.** כי כשר והגון הוא שימלוך, כי גם במלכותו הוא נהפך ממנהג השררה ומקטין עצמו אצל החכמים כמדת הרשים; וכן (איוב יא:יב) ועיר פרא אדם יולד — שיהפך וישתנה לו ממה שהיה כעיר פרא ויעשה אדם: **נולד.** נעשה, ולשון הוה הוא: (טו) **ראיתי את־כל־החיים וגו׳.** מצאתי במדרש הספר הזה (ע׳ קהלת זוטא) — זה דור המבול, שנאמר בהם (בראשית ו:יט) ומכל־החי: **עם הילד השני. אשר יתקיים** תחת אותו הדור, שהם נח ובניו:

(טז) **אין־קץ לכל־העם.** פרים ורבים היו יותר מדאי, כמו שנאמר (איוב כא:ח־יא) זרעם נכון לפניהם — אשה מתעברת ויולדת לשלשה ימים (בראשית

13–16 / People prefer glamor to truth

13] Better a poor but wise child . . . In a man-made society where people are not guided by absolute truths, there

13] Better a poor but wise child than an old but foolish king who no longer knows how to exercise caution.

14] Even if from the prison he came forth to rule; even if he were born a pauper in his own kingdom.

15] I observed that all the living under the sun were with the youthful successor who stepped into his place.

16] There was no limit to the number of people for whom he was the acknowledged leader. And

are many vanities. One of these is the search for glamor even at the expense of truth. Koheleth cites the case, real or hypothetical, of the young, talented, and wise commoner who is chosen by an overwhelming popularity to become king and is later rejected because he is not of royal lineage.

14] EVEN IF FROM THE PRISON . . . Even if he has to come out of prison or from a family that has served terms in prison, he may yet be a potentially great leader.

EVEN IF . . . BORN A PAUPER . . . Though his parents may have belonged to the poor class, he may have been born wise and talented and destined to the crown.

15] I OBSERVED THAT ALL THE LIVING . . . The choice of the young one, who appeared as a child compared to the old monarch, was so overwhelming that it seemed that all the living were on his side.

16] THERE WAS NO LIMIT . . . He performed so well that all acknowledged his superior leadership.

לֹא יִשְׂמְחוּ־בוֹ כִּי־גַם־זֶה הֶבֶל וְרַעְיוֹן רוּחַ:
יז] שְׁמֹר רגליך [רַגְלְךָ] כַּאֲשֶׁר תֵּלֵךְ אֶל־בֵּית הָאֱלֹהִים וְקָרוֹב
לִשְׁמֹעַ מִתֵּת הַכְּסִילִים זָבַח כִּי־אֵינָם יוֹדְעִים לַעֲשׂוֹת רָע:

רבה לו א, וע׳ ויק״ר פ״ה), ישלחו כצאן עויליהם: **לכל אשר־היה לפניהם.** אין קץ לכל טוב שהיה לפניהם, והכל אבד (שם: יג) וברגע שאול יחתו; **גם האחרונים** — דור הפלגה, **לא ישמחו** גם הם בטוב הניתן בידם, **כי־גם־זה.** סופו של הבל ורעיון רוח, כאשר אדם מהלך אחרי יצרו:

(יז) **שמר רגלך כאשר תלך אל־בית האלהים.** היאך תלך; אם תביא תודה ונדבת שלמים, הוא הטוב, ושמר עצמך שלא תצטרך לילך בהבאת חטאות ואשמות: **וקרוב** הוי **לשמע** דברי הקדוש ברוך הוא, והוא טוב וקרוב להקדוש ברוך הוא, **מתת הכסילים זבח.** שיחטא ויביא קרבן: **כי־אינם יודעים לעשות רע.** אין הכסיל מבין שהוא עושה רע לעצמו (ע׳ ברכות כג ע״א).

THE NEXT GENERATION WILL NOT REJOICE IN HIM. Though the young leader had proved himself capable beyond doubt, the next generation demanded a return to a monarch of royal descent. Such is the tendency among men—to seek glamor and royal lineage even if efficiency is sacrificed in the process.

THIS TOO IS VANITY AND CHASING OF WIND. The forsaking of wisdom and talent for glamor can only lead to corrupt government and national catastrophe. But these are the vanities of men. People who do not seek truth, end up chasing wind.

17 / The wise man is circumspect

17] TREAD CAREFULLY . . . Fools will seek glamor rather than truth; they will avoid outright evil but are easy prey for what appears superficially good. In consequence, the fool

yet the next generation will not rejoice in him. This, too, is vanity and chasing of wind.

17] Tread carefully when you would enter the house of Elohim; it is better to hearken than to offer sacrifices like the fools who do not know to perform outright evil.

is unwittingly led into sin and is always offering sacrifices to repair his indiscretion and always begging forgiveness.

The wise man is expected to be more circumspect and to avoid what is superficially good but may lead to evil.

WHEN YOU WOULD ENTER THE HOUSE OF ELOHIM . . . To enter the house of Elohim, to be near Elohim, one must avoid evil in all its forms. Koheleth warns in the spirit of caution spoken by Samuel when he reproved Saul, "To hearken is better than to sacrifice" (I Samuel 15:22). Elohim prefers to be obeyed rather than to be appeased. He expects the wise and knowledgeable to guard themselves against evil.

LIKE THE FOOLS WHO DO NOT KNOW . . . "Do not know" in the sense of "not being able" as in the phrase, "able to play" (I Samuel 16:18). The fools do not know, that is, they are not able to perform, outright evil. But they are easily misled by what appears pure and pious on the surface. When the fools discover that they have strayed, they offer sacrifices to redeem themselves.

The wise individual is expected to hearken and avoid the evil that is concealed from the eye of the fool. The wise man knows that what leads to evil is also evil. He cannot redeem himself like the fool through sacrifices.

Chapter 5

GREED

They are greedy dogs
which can never have enough.

Isaiah

א] אַל־תְּבַהֵל עַל־פִּיךָ וְלִבְּךָ אַל־יְמַהֵר לְהוֹצִיא דָבָר לִפְנֵי הָאֱלֹהִים כִּי הָאֱלֹהִים בַּשָּׁמַיִם וְאַתָּה עַל־הָאָרֶץ עַל־כֵּן יִהְיוּ דְבָרֶיךָ מְעַטִּים:

(א) **להוציא דבר לפני האלהים.** לדבר קשה כלפי מעלה, **כי הוא בשמים ואתה על־הארץ.** ואפילו חלש מלמעלה וגבור מלמטה — אימת חלש על הגבור, וכל שכן גבור למעלה וחלש למטה (ספרי האזינו לב:ו):

1-6 / The vanity of words

1] The present verse may be related to the final verse in Chapter 4. It may be (a) advice to the individual who enters the "house of Elohim" on how to be circumspect when offering prayer, or (b) it may be a warning to be careful with words which on the surface appear harmless but may result in much strife and suffering.

Do not rush to speak . . . In offering prayers and supplications to Elohim, one must carefully bethink himself and choose his words.

nor permit your heart . . . The heart has a tendency to wander off in many directions if uncontrolled. When one prays before Elohim one should organize one's thoughts and choose one's words. In fact, the Rabbis recommend spending some time in serious contemplation before uttering prayer.

for Elohim is in heaven . . . Though one prays to Elohim as though he were speaking to Him directly, a psychological distance must be maintained; the spatial distance is merely symbolic. This precaution is necessary to that a sense of the "fear of Elohim" will prevail. Though Elohim is always near-

1] Do not rush to speak, nor permit your heart to hasten to utter words before Elohim, for Elohim is in heaven and you are on earth. Therefore, let your words be few.

by, one must picture Him in the heavens above in order to avoid excessive familiarity and anthropomorphism.

LET YOUR WORDS BE FEW. A few well-chosen words in prayer can be more effective than a long verbose supplication.

Alternate Commentary:

1] DO NOT RUSH TO SPEAK . . . Koheleth cautions us in the spirit of his father, David, "Guard your tongue from evil" (Psalms 34:14).

Much of the trouble that the human race suffers from has its root in the evil tongue: gossip, slander, false rumor, and defamation of character. Therefore, do not rush to speak. Bethink yourself and weigh the effect of your words.

NOR PERMIT YOUR HEART . . . The heart is governed by emotions and has a tendency to hasten to conclusions which have little basis in fact. Hasty judgments are frequently erroneous, yet may serve as a basis for unwarranted bitterness and feuds as well as misunderstandings.

BEFORE ELOHIM . . . Even if you reach your hasty conclusions on your own or relate them only to a selected circle, they are still evil. Elohim is near you and He knows and hears your evil thoughts and evil tongue.

FOR ELOHIM IS IN HEAVEN . . . And the fear of Elohim should therefore cause you to examine more closely your hasty con-

ב] כִּי בָּא הַחֲלוֹם בְּרֹב עִנְיָן וְקוֹל כְּסִיל בְּרֹב דְּבָרִים׃
ג] כַּאֲשֶׁר תִּדֹּר נֶדֶר לֵאלֹהִים אַל־תְּאַחֵר לְשַׁלְּמוֹ כִּי אֵין חֵפֶץ
בַּכְּסִילִים אֵת אֲשֶׁר־תִּדֹּר שַׁלֵּם׃
ד] טוֹב אֲשֶׁר לֹא־תִדֹּר מִשֶּׁתִּדּוֹר וְלֹא תְשַׁלֵּם׃
ה] אַל־תִּתֵּן אֶת־פִּיךָ לַחֲטִיא אֶת־בְּשָׂרֶךָ וְאַל־תֹּאמַר לִפְנֵי
הַמַּלְאָךְ כִּי שְׁגָגָה הִיא לָמָּה יִקְצֹף הָאֱלֹהִים עַל־קוֹלֶךָ וְחִבֵּל
אֶת־מַעֲשֵׂה יָדֶיךָ׃

(ב) **כי בא החלום ברב ענין.** כי דרך החלום לבוא ברוב הרהורים, שאדם מעיין ומהרהר ביום, ודרך קול כסיל לבוא ברב דברים, כי בהרבותו דברים מוציא קול של כסילות מפיו כי לא יחדל פשע, לכך אני אומר יהיו דבריך מעטים: (ג) **אין חפץ בכסילים.** אין חפץ לפני הקדוש ברוך הוא ברשעים הנודרים ואין משלמים: (ה) **אל־תתן את־פיך** בנדר **לחטיא את־בשרך.** שיפקוד העון על בניך (שבועות לט ע"א): **ואל־תאמר לפני המלאך** — שליח הבא לתובעך, צדקה שפסקת ברבים **כי שגגה היא.** בשגגה פסקתיה, כסבור הייתי שתהיה יכולת בידי ליתן: **וחבל את־מעשה ידיך.** מצוות שהיו בידיך שעשית כבר אבדתם. כך נדרש במדרש

clusions. One must weigh very carefully the circumstances under which an action was performed; one must know all the facts surrounding an incident before making judgment.

LET YOUR WORDS BE FEW. Therefore, every word uttered about another person must be pondered and examined as to its veracity and its effect.

2] JUST AS THE DREAM COMES . . . Just as the dream comes with a multitude of subjects in complete disarray and in illogical order, so the fool speaks a multitude of words which frequently contain disconnected thoughts lacking logical sequence. But though the dream is harmless, the unguarded words of the fool may cause much evil and anguish.

2] For just as the dream comes with a multitude of subjects, so does the fool speak with a multitude of words.

3] When you make a vow to Elohim, do not delay fulfilling it, for He has no desire in fools. Therefore, always be sure that you make good your pledge.

4] Better not to vow at all than to vow and not to fulfill.

5] Do not permit your mouth to bring your flesh into guilt; nor say before the angel that it was an error. Why should Elohim be angered by your voice, and destroy the work of your hands?

3] WHEN YOU HAVE MADE A VOW ... The superfluity of words is likely to lead to the misuse of vows. When people are in trouble, there is a tendency to vow. While this has some virtue, it may also lead to empty promises and habitual insincerity. In time of trouble a person may sincerely mean to keep his vow, but when times become better, the frail human frequently forgets the pledge he made during his suffering; in the fat years, he forgets the lean years.

4] BETTER NOT TO VOW ... Better to perform the good deed and trust in Elohim than to make a vow and possibly suffer the consequences of a pledge unredeemed.

5] YOUR MOUTH TO BRING YOUR FLESH ... The kingly family suffered greatly from the slander of the loose tongue. Koheleth expresses a family tradition when he warns of the harm that a careless mouth may bring to the whole body:

ו] כִּי בְרֹב חֲלֹמוֹת וַהֲבָלִים וּדְבָרִים הַרְבֵּה כִּי אֶת־הָאֱלֹהִים
יְרָא׃

(מדרש תהלים נב:א): על־קולך. בשביל קולך: (ו) **כי ברב חלמות וגו'.** אשר כל מה שיאמרו לך חלומות ונביאי הבל ודברים הרבה לפרוש מאת המקום, **כי את־האלהים ירא.** הרי כי משמש בלשון אלא; אל תשמע אל החלומות, אלא את האלהים ירא:

> Who is the man who desires life
> And loves days, that he may see good?
> Then guard your tongue from evil
> And your lips from speaking guile.
> (Psalms 34:13–14)

Just a little bit of slander can sometimes bring in its wake a lifetime of pain and misery.

DESTROY THE WORK OF YOUR HANDS. After the harm was done it does not help much to say, "It was an error." It is therefore important to weigh one's words and to evaluate the consequences of a remark before making it.

Koheleth considers the evil tongue one of the worst of crimes, one punishable by destruction. His father, David, said before him, "Whoever slanders his neighbor in secret, him will I destroy" (Psalms 101:5).

6] IN HIS MULTITUDE OF DREAMS . . . Koheleth expounds here on this most difficult task of controlling one's thoughts — even one's dreams. The frail human is besieged by vanities, evil thoughts and an almost irrepressible desire to express

6] In his multitude of dreams and vanities and in his multitude of words, the only thing for a man to do is to fear Elohim.

himself in words. Yet he is asked to control his thoughts and his speech.

How relaxing it is to vent one's anger in speech; how relieving it is to slander; how comforting it is to make a vow; how heroic to express oneself in filthy language. Yet man is asked to avoid these things if he would avoid self-destruction.

TO FEAR ELOHIM. The temptation to speak evil is so great that only the fear of Elohim can hold man back. To banish the evil tongue one must first banish the evil thought. Do not say that even if man cannot speak evil, he can think evil and no one will know the difference. Elohim knows even when man only thinks evil.

If one thinks evil it is almost impossible not to express evil. Hence the only deterrent to the evil tongue and the evil thought is the "fear of Elohim." Man must act like man, not only in the presence of others, but also when he is alone with his thoughts. The knowledge that Elohim is always present and knows all his thoughts will help man to transform his mind from a receptacle for trash to a respectable inner sanctum.

ז] אִם־עֹשֶׁק רָשׁ וְגֵזֶל מִשְׁפָּט וָצֶדֶק תִּרְאֶה בַמְּדִינָה אַל־תִּתְמַהּ
עַל־הַחֵפֶץ כִּי גָבֹהַּ מֵעַל גָּבֹהַּ שֹׁמֵר וּגְבֹהִים עֲלֵיהֶם׃
ח] וְיִתְרוֹן אֶרֶץ בַּכֹּל הִיא [הוּא] מֶלֶךְ לְשָׂדֶה נֶעֱבָד׃

(ז) **אם־עשק רש וגזל משפט וצדק וגו׳. אם... תראה במדינה** שהם עושקים את הרשים וגוזלים את המשפט ואת הצדק, **אל־תתמה** על חפצו של מקום כשיביא עליהם רעה, **כי גבה מעל גבה שמר** ורואה את מעשיהם, **וגבהים** יש עליהם העושים שליחותו של מקום וידם תקיפה ליפרע מהם: **וגזל משפט.** גזל של משפט; לפי שהוא דבוק (הוא) נקוד גזל פתח קטן, שאם לא היה דבוק היה נקוד גזל קמץ. ענין אחר, **אם... תראה** שהם עושקים רשים וגוזלים משפט, ורואה אתה צדק בא לעיר, שהקדוש ברוך הוא משפיע להם טובה ואינו נפרע מהם — **אל־תתמה** על חפצו של מקום, כי כן דרכו להאריך אפו, **כי גבה מעל גבה שמר** — ממתין עד שתתמלא סאתם, **וגבהים** יש לו **עליהם** ליפרע מהם בבא עת פקודתם, כמו (איוב יד: טז) לא־תשמר על־חטאתי, (ישעיה כו: ב) שמר אמנים, (בראשית לז: יא) שמר את־הדבר: (ח) **ויתרון ארץ (בכל הוא).** ויתרון של יושבי הארץ, שהם מתגאים ומכעיסים למקום, **בכל הוא.** בכל דבר הוא עושה שליחותו ליפרע ואפילו על ידי יתושין, כדרך שעשה לטיטוס (גיטין נו ע״ב): **מלך לשדה נעבד.** הקדוש ברוך הוא נעשה פועל לציון, לתבוע עלבונה ממחריביה ולשלם שכרה לבוניה (ע׳ קה״ר):

7-8 / Corruption and injustice in man-made government

7] IF YOU OBSERVE . . . THE OPPRESSION OF THE POOR . . . Koheleth now turns to another form of injustice — the corrupt state. If you find the poor oppressed, the weak taken advantage of, and justice perverted in favor of the wealthy, then know that this stems from corruption in the higher

7] If you observe, in the state, the oppression of the poor and the perversion of justice and righteousness, do not be astonished by the fact, for each official has one above him and there are still higher ones above them.

8] The advantage of possession of land is sought by all; even a king becomes a slave to soil.

echelons. Here the heads of state are stricken with that common malady — the pursuit of money and possessions.

FOR EACH OFFICIAL HAS ONE ABOVE HIM . . . Generally, it is not the lowly clerk who is to blame but the one who is supposed to supervise him.

AND THERE ARE STILL HIGHER ONES ABOVE THEM. The corruption probably ascends all the way to the top.

8] POSSESSION OF LAND IS SOUGHT BY ALL . . . The temptation for graft is great. Corrupt clerks will accept gratuities in the hope that some day they, too, will be able to own real property.

EVEN A KING BECOMES A SLAVE TO SOIL. Corruption often goes to the very top, where the king, too, will pervert justice and take advantage of the weak in order to expropriate wealth for his personal benefit.

ט] אֹהֵב כֶּסֶף לֹא־יִשְׂבַּע כֶּסֶף וּמִי־אֹהֵב בֶּהָמוֹן לֹא תְבוּאָה
גַּם־זֶה הָבֶל׃
י] בִּרְבוֹת הַטּוֹבָה רַבּוּ אוֹכְלֶיהָ וּמַה־כִּשְׁרוֹן לִבְעָלֶיהָ כִּי אִם־
ראית [רְאוּת] עֵינָיו׃
יא] מְתוּקָה שְׁנַת הָעֹבֵד אִם־מְעַט וְאִם־הַרְבֵּה יֹאכֵל וְהַשָּׂבָע

(ט) **אהב כסף לא־ישבע כסף.** אוהב מצוות לא ישבע מהם, **ומי־אהב בהמון** — מצוות רבות, **לא תבואה** — ואין באחד מהם מצוה מסויימת וניכרת, כגון בנין בית המקדש ובית הכנסת וספר תורה נאה, **גם־זה הבל**; כך נדרשים שני מקראות הללו במדרש (ויקרא רבה פרשה כב). ועוד פנים אחרים הגונים, אך זה הקדמתי לפי שהוא מענין 'וגבהים עליהם' שסמכן הכתוב יחד. דבר אחר, **ויתרון ארץ בכל הוא.** שכר עבודת האדמה חשוב הוא על הכל, שאפילו הוא **מלך,** צריך הוא להיות **נעבד לשדה**; אם עשתה הארץ פירות יש לו מה יאכל, ואם לאו מת ברעב: **אהב כסף לא־ישבע כסף.** לא יאכל כסף, **ומי־אהב בהמון,** בממון, **לא תבואה,** שאינו אוסף לו פירות — **גם זה הבל.** דבר אחר, **ויתרון ארץ בכל הוא.** שכרן של ישראל **בכל** דברי תורה **הוא,** בין במקרא בין במשנה בין בתלמוד; **מלך לשדה נעבד.** מלך במקרא ובמשנה עודנו צריך **להיות נעבד** לבעל תלמוד, שהוא מסדר לפניו הוראות איסור והיתר, טומאה וטהרה ודינין; **אהב כסף.** אוהב תורה אינו שבע בה, **ומי־אהב בהמון** — תורה — **לא תבואה.** שיש לו מקרא ומשנה ואין לו תלמוד, מה הנאה יש לו? כל אלו בויקרא רבה (שם): (י) **ברבות הטובה.** כשישראל מטיבין מעשיהם: **רבו אוכליה.** מתן שכר המצות: **ומה־כשרון לבעליה.** להקדוש ברוך הוא בכל הטבת מעשיהם: **כי אם־ראות עיניו.** שרואה שהם כפופים לו, ונחת רוח לפניו שאמר ונעשה רצונו. וכן לעניין הקרבנות, **ברבות הטובה** (**רבו אוכליה**). שמביאים נדבות הרבה, **רבו** הכהנים **אוכליה, ומה־כשרון לבעליה.** לפני הקדוש ברוך הוא: **כי אם־ראות עיניו.** שאמר ונעשה רצונו (מנחות קי ע"א): (יא) **מתוקה שנת העבד.**

9–16 / Pursuit of wealth — road to unhappiness

9] He who loves money ... When one's aim in life is money and possessions, then it matters not whether he be rich or poor, proletarian or bourgeois, he will never be satisfied with what he has. The glitter of what he might acquire makes what he already possesses look dull. He is also liable to succumb to any temptation or scheme that will help him get rich quick.

9] He who loves money will never have enough money, nor will he who loves abundance be satisfied with the productivity. This too is vanity.

10] As wealth increases, so do those who would consume it. And what has the possessor's ability netted him other than a temporary glance at the wealth?

11] Sweet is the sleep of the workingman, whether he has eaten little or much; but the satiety of

THIS TOO IS VANITY. Koheleth never tires of pointing out that many an individual's unhappiness is due to his slave-like attachment to the pursuit of money. This ceaseless devotion to the service of the golden calf robs man of time for enjoyment and for the pursuit of higher values, thus reducing life to vanity.

10] AS WEALTH INCREASES . . . The increase of wealth does not always bring with it satisfaction or peace of mind. On the contrary, the possessor seems only to gather more relatives, friends, dependents and other factors whose objective it is to consume that wealth.

WHAT HAS THE POSSESSOR'S ABILITY . . . After applying so much time planning and working to acquire the wealth, after denying himself joys and comforts — even life itself — in order to "make money," all he now has is a very temporary pleasant feeling aroused by a glance at his wealth. Soon it will belong to others.

11] SWEET IS THE SLEEP OF THE WORKINGMAN . . . The man who earns comparatively little, but who is satisfied with what he earns, is more at peace with the world than the man who is always under tension because he wants more.

לֶעָשִׁיר אֵינֶנּוּ מַנִּיחַ לוֹ לִישׁוֹן׃
יב] יֵשׁ רָעָה חוֹלָה רָאִיתִי תַּחַת הַשָּׁמֶשׁ עֹשֶׁר שָׁמוּר לִבְעָלָיו
לְרָעָתוֹ׃
יג] וְאָבַד הָעֹשֶׁר הַהוּא בְּעִנְיַן רָע וְהוֹלִיד בֵּן וְאֵין בְּיָדוֹ מְאוּמָה׃
יד] כַּאֲשֶׁר יָצָא מִבֶּטֶן אִמּוֹ עָרוֹם יָשׁוּב לָלֶכֶת כְּשֶׁבָּא וּמְאוּמָה
לֹא־יִשָּׂא בַעֲמָלוֹ שֶׁיֹּלֵךְ בְּיָדוֹ׃
טו] וְגַם־זֹה רָעָה חוֹלָה כָּל־עֻמַּת שֶׁבָּא כֵּן יֵלֵךְ וּמַה־יִּתְרוֹן לוֹ
שֶׁיַּעֲמֹל לָרוּחַ׃

עובד האדמה ישן וערבה שנתו עליו, בין שהוא אוכל מעט ובין שהוא אוכל הרבה, כי כבר הורגל בכך: **והשבע לעשיר איננו מניח לו לישון.** ושובע נכסים של עשיר בעל פרקמטיאות הרבה אינו מניח לו לישון, כל הלילה מהרהר בהן. דבר אחר, מתוקה שנת העבד את האלהים, **אם־מעט** ימי שניו **ואם־הרבה** ימי שניו, יאכל שכרו המועט כמרובה; משה פירנס את ישראל ארבעים שנה ושמואל הנביא פירנסם עשר שנים ושקלן הכתוב זה כזה, שנאמר (תהלים צט:ו) משה ואהרן בכהניו ושמואל בקראי שמו וגו׳. כך נדרש בתנחומא (כי תשא ג); **והשבע לעשיר** — בעל שמועות — **איננו מניח לו לישון** בקבר, שנאמר (שיר השירים ז:י) דובב שפתי ישנים — כל תלמיד חכם שאומרים דבר שמועה מפיו, שפתותיו דובבות בקבר (יבמות צז ע״א; ושם): (יב) **עשר שמור לבעליו לרעתו.** כעשרו של קרח, שעל ידי כן נתגאה וירד לשאול (פסחים קיט ע״א, ע״ש): (יג) **ואין בידו מאומה.** אף זכות אבות: (יד) **ומאומה לא־ישא בעמלו.** כשימות, לא ישא בידו שום זכות צדקה שעשה בממונו בחייו: (טו) **כל־**

The satiety of the rich man . . . Just as an overstuffed stomach does not permit one to sleep, so does the surfeit of wealth disturb one's peace of mind. Besides the tensions caused by the endless desire for more, anxiety possesses the rich man because of his need to care properly for so many expensive and varied possessions.

12] There is a grievous evil . . . Again Koheleth deplores man's devoting the best years of his life to the pursuit of money. Man's turning from need to greed is the greatest source of his unhappiness. In verses 12–16, Koheleth la-the rich man does not permit him to sleep.

12] There is a grievous evil I have seen under the sun — wealth acquired by its owner to his own detriment.

13] If that wealth is lost by an unfortunate circumstance, and should he beget a son, the father will have nothing to bequeath to him.

14] As the father came from his mother's womb, so shall he return naked, and he shall carry in hand nothing of worth for all his toil.

15] This, too, is a grievous evil — as he came, so shall he depart; and what advantage was there for him in laboring for the wind?

ments the individual who denies himself everything in order to accumulate wealth and then loses that wealth through some tragic mishap.

TO HIS OWN DETRIMENT. In the end he wasted a lifetime, for he lost his wealth and spent the rest of his days in agony.

13] THE FATHER WILL HAVE NOTHING TO BEQUEATH . . . Even the common excuse that he worked in order to provide an inheritance sounds like an empty phrase when that wealth is gone.

14] AS THE FATHER CAME . . . His one excuse for his slaving for the golden calf gone, the father has no explanation for his living. He was born naked and now takes nothing with him and leaves nothing behind.

15] AND WHAT ADVANTAGE . . . What did this father live

טז] גַּם כָּל־יָמָיו בַּחֹשֶׁךְ יֹאכֵל וְכָעַס הַרְבֵּה וְחָלְיוֹ וָקָצֶף׃

עמת שבא אותו הממון, כן ילך : (טז) וחליו. כמו וחולי, והוי״ו יתירה כמו וי״ו
של (תהלים קד : כ) חיתו־יער :

for? He had no pleasure out of life and did not even provide an inheritance.

16] HE ATE IN DARKNESS . . . Koheleth pictures the depths to which man sinks in his search for money. There is no true

16] All his days, too, he ate in darkness and suffered much vexation, sickness, and anger.

cheer in his life, even at mealtime. He eats in darkness; he is constantly worried about financial problems; he is angered by financial losses. He may suffer illness because of prolonged anxiety over money matters.

יז] הִנֵּה אֲשֶׁר־רָאִיתִי אָנִי טוֹב אֲשֶׁר־יָפֶה לֶאֱכוֹל וְלִשְׁתּוֹת
וְלִרְאוֹת טוֹבָה בְּכָל־עֲמָלוֹ שֶׁיַּעֲמֹל תַּחַת־הַשֶּׁמֶשׁ מִסְפַּר
יְמֵי־חַיָּו אֲשֶׁר־נָתַן־לוֹ הָאֱלֹהִים כִּי־הוּא חֶלְקוֹ:
יח] גַּם כָּל־הָאָדָם אֲשֶׁר נָתַן־לוֹ הָאֱלֹהִים עֹשֶׁר וּנְכָסִים וְהִשְׁלִיטוֹ
לֶאֱכֹל מִמֶּנּוּ וְלָשֵׂאת אֶת־חֶלְקוֹ וְלִשְׂמֹחַ בַּעֲמָלוֹ זֹה מַתַּת
אֱלֹהִים הִיא:
יט] כִּי לֹא הַרְבֵּה יִזְכֹּר אֶת־יְמֵי חַיָּיו כִּי הָאֱלֹהִים מַעֲנֶה בְּשִׂמְחַת
לִבּוֹ:

(יז) **לאכול ולשתות ולראות טובה.** לעסוק בתורה שהיא לקח טוב (ע׳ להלן ח: טו ורש״י שם), ואל יקבץ הון רב, אלא בחלק הניתן לו ישמח, **כי־הוא חלקו:** (יח) **והשליטו לאכל ממנו** בחייו **ולשאת את־חלקו** במותו, שיזכהו לעסוק בתורה ובמצוות בחייו כדי שיקבל שכר: (יט) **כי לא הרבה.** שאין אורך ימים בעולם הזה: **יזכר את־ימי חייו.** כי מעט הם ולא הרבה, ולמה יטרח לאסוף הון? יטרח בדבר העומד לו לעולם הבא בחייו: **כי האלהים מענה** וגו׳. הקדוש ברוך הוא עדות קבועה לזה לעולם: **בשמחת לבו.** ששמח לעשות טוב בחייו. וראיתי במדרש (ע׳ קה״ר) — זה אלקנה, שמדריך את ישראל לעלות לשילה ברגלים, ובדרך שמעלה אותן לשנה זו לא היה מעלה אותן לשנה האחרת, כדי לפרסם הדבר ולהרגילם; לפיכך ייחסו הכתוב (שמואל א׳ א: ג) ועלה האיש ההוא מעירו וגומר. ואומר אני שהמדרש הזה סוף המקרא הוא, **כי האלהים מענה בשמחת לבו** — זה אלקנה, שקבע לו הקדוש ברוך הוא עדות בכתובים והעיד עליו (שמואל א, א: ג) ועלה האיש ההוא מעירו: **מענה.** נקוד פתח קטן, לכך אני מפרשו שם דבר, כמו (איוב לב: ה) כי אין מענה בפי שלשת האנשים: **בשמחת לבו.** שהיה שמח ברגל:

17–19 / Rejoicing in one's portion is the key to happiness

17] EAT AND DRINK AND DERIVE SATISFACTION . . . For the fourth time (see 2:24, 3:13, 3:22) Koheleth repeats the major theme: man was born to enjoy life, to rejoice with what he possesses and to be contented with his lot.

UNDER THE SUN . . . Even the man who is stricken with the "under-the-sun" philosophy would find greater enjoyment in

17] From the above considerations, I have concluded that it is good, even commendable, for man to eat and drink and derive satisfaction from his labor, under the sun, during the numbered days Elohim has granted him, for that is his portion.

18] Indeed, when Elohim has provided man with wealth and possessions and enabled him to eat thereof, to take his share thereof, and enjoy his labor — this should be considered a gift of Elohim.

19] For man should remember that his days are not many, and Elohim provides for the joy in his heart.

living if he could learn to be satisfied with his share of the wealth.

18] WHEN ELOHIM HAS PROVIDED ... Everything that man possesses — life, health, wealth and wisdom — all are provided by Elohim.

ENABLED HIM TO EAT THEREOF ... Alas, there are some unfortunates who do not have all of the above. Therefore, he who has them and is able to enjoy them should be grateful for his good fortune.

A GIFT OF ELOHIM. Enjoy your possessions, enjoy your labor — but realize that it is a gift of Elohim. The ability to enjoy, the ability to be satisfied with what one has, the ability to free oneself from slavery — all are gifts of Elohim.

19] HIS DAYS ARE NOT MANY ... Man's span of life is a small one. It is a pity to waste that life in an endless pursuit of material gain.

AND ELOHIM PROVIDES FOR THE JOY . . . Elohim gives man the opportunity and the ability to enjoy living. It is a shame that man should not do his utmost to enjoy the few short years that he has to live.

Chapter 6

HAPPINESS

The righteous eats to sate himself,
but the belly of the wicked never has enough.
Proverbs

א] יֵשׁ רָעָה אֲשֶׁר רָאִיתִי תַּחַת הַשָּׁמֶשׁ וְרַבָּה הִיא עַל־הָאָדָם׃

ב] אִישׁ אֲשֶׁר יִתֶּן־לוֹ הָאֱלֹהִים עֹשֶׁר וּנְכָסִים וְכָבוֹד וְאֵינֶנּוּ חָסֵר
לְנַפְשׁוֹ מִכֹּל אֲשֶׁר־יִתְאַוֶּה וְלֹא־יַשְׁלִיטֶנּוּ הָאֱלֹהִים לֶאֱכֹל
מִמֶּנּוּ כִּי אִישׁ נָכְרִי יֹאכְלֶנּוּ זֶה הֶבֶל וָחֳלִי רָע הוּא׃

ג] אִם־יוֹלִיד אִישׁ מֵאָה וְשָׁנִים רַבּוֹת יִחְיֶה וְרַב שֶׁיִּהְיוּ יְמֵי־שָׁנָיו
וְנַפְשׁוֹ לֹא־תִשְׂבַּע מִן־הַטּוֹבָה וְגַם־קְבוּרָה לֹא־הָיְתָה לּוֹ
אָמַרְתִּי טוֹב מִמֶּנּוּ הַנָּפֶל׃

(א) **ורבה היא על־האדם.** בהרבה בני אדם היא נוהגת: (ב) **עשר ונכסים.** לפי פשוטו כמשמעו: **ולא־ישליטנו האלהים (לאכל ממנו)** שיהא שמח בחלקו למצוא קורת רוח בעשרו, כי שואף לעשוק ולהרבות הון, כענין שנאמר (חבקוק ב:ה) והוא כמות ולא ישבע, וגם לא ישליטנו לעשות צדקה **לאכול הימנו** לעתיד, **ואיש נכרי** יטול אותו ממון ויעשה בו צדקה ויהנה ממנו. ומדרש אגדה (ע׳ ירוש׳ הוריות פ״ג ה״ה) בדברי תורה: **עשר ונכסים וכבוד.** מקרא, משנה ואגדה: **ולא־ישליטנו.** שלא זכה לתלמוד ומתוך כך אין הנאה ממנו בשום דבר הוראה: **כי איש נכרי יאכלנו.** זה בעל התלמוד: (ג) **אם־יוליד איש מאה** בנים, **ורב** הון וכל טוב שיהיו ימי־שניו שלו. ורב לשון די — די לכל טובה. ונפשו **לא־תשבע** מאותה הטובה, שאינו שמח בחלקו להתקרר רוחו במה שבידו, וגם־קבורה **לא־היתה** לו. פעמים שנהרג, וכלבים אוכלים אותו; וכל הדברים האלו נמצאו באחאב (ע׳ קה״ר), שהוליד בנים הרבה וממונו הרבה והיה חומד של אחרים ולא מצא קורת רוח בממונו, וכלבים אכלוהו — **טוב ממנו**

1–6 / Life without enjoyment is meaningless

1] THERE IS EVIL . . . After having told man, at the close of the last chapter, that "Elohim provides for the joy in his heart," Koheleth deplores the evil and the vanity in a life where man possesses wealth but does not enjoy it. Man may fail to enjoy life because he willfully enslaves himself in an endless pursuit of wealth or he may be denied the right to

CHAPTER SIX

1] There is evil I have seen under the sun and it weighs heavily on man.

2] Elohim grants a man wealth, possessions and honor; he lacks nothing that his heart desires; but Elohim does not permit him to eat thereof, for it is destined for another; this is vanity, an evil plague.

3] Even if a man should beget a hundred children and live many years, yea, never even to be buried, but he should not enjoy the good in this world — I say that the stillborn child is better off than he.

enjoy the fruit of his labor because he has sinned and failed to repent. Even a wise and intelligent person may doom himself to unhappiness if he should succumb to envy and greed.

IT WEIGHS HEAVILY ON MAN. Failure to enjoy life, failure to count one's blessings, takes all the meaning out of living.

2] ELOHIM DOES NOT PERMIT HIM . . . Sometimes man's sin is so outrageous that Elohim no longer permits him to exercise his option of enjoyment. See the close of Chapter 2 (verse 26).

3] BUT HE SHOULD NOT ENJOY THE GOOD . . . This is the worst evil that can befall man. Man could possess everything good and could live many years but if he does not enjoy life then he merely exists; worse — he is self-destructive.

ד כִּי־בַהֶבֶל בָּא וּבַחֹשֶׁךְ יֵלֵךְ וּבַחֹשֶׁךְ שְׁמוֹ יְכֻסֶּה׃
ה גַּם־שֶׁמֶשׁ לֹא־רָאָה וְלֹא יָדָע נַחַת לָזֶה מִזֶּה׃
ו וְאִלּוּ חָיָה אֶלֶף שָׁנִים פַּעֲמַיִם וְטוֹבָה לֹא רָאָה הֲלֹא אֶל־
מָקוֹם אֶחָד הַכֹּל הוֹלֵךְ׃

(ד) **כי הנפל בהבל בא** והלך ולא ראה טובה ולא נתאוה לה ואין לו להצטער: הנפל של אשה [זונה], (ו) **ואלו חיה**, ואם חיה אלפים שנה מה יתרון לו, הואיל **וטובה לא ראה**, הלא סופו לשוב אל העפר כשאר העניים:

4] ITS NAME IS COVERED IN DARKNESS. The child may have no chance to be named. Even if named, it is readily forgotten and the whole episode is a transient one.

5] HIS LOT IS BETTER THAN THE MAN'S . . . He has not seen life; he has not had to suffer the problems and vexations of the average individual.

4] The stillborn child comes in vanity and departs in darkness and its name is covered in darkness.
5] Though it never sees or knows sunlight, its lot is better than the man's —
6] even if the man live a thousand years twice over, since the man derives no enjoyment. Do they not all go to one place?

6] All go to one place. To have lived and not to have enjoyed life is in no way better than to be stillborn. Certainly, the end is the same — all go to one place.

ז] כָּל־עֲמַל הָאָדָם לְפִיהוּ וְגַם־הַנֶּפֶשׁ לֹא תִמָּלֵא׃
ח] כִּי מַה־יּוֹתֵר לֶחָכָם מִן־הַכְּסִיל מַה־לֶּעָנִי יוֹדֵעַ לַהֲלֹךְ נֶגֶד
הַחַיִּים׃
ט] טוֹב מַרְאֵה עֵינַיִם מֵהֲלָךְ־נָפֶשׁ גַּם־זֶה הֶבֶל וּרְעוּת רוּחַ׃
י] מַה־שֶּׁהָיָה כְּבָר נִקְרָא שְׁמוֹ וְנוֹדָע אֲשֶׁר־הוּא אָדָם וְלֹא־
יוּכַל לָדִין עִם שהתקיף [שֶׁתַּקִּיף] מִמֶּנּוּ׃

(ז) **כל־עמל האדם** בשביל **פיהו** הוא, שיהנה ויאכל בעולם הזה (והבא), וזה לא נהנה בחייו; **וגם־הנפש לא תמלא**. בתמיה; כלומר, וזה — אפילו תאותו לא מלאה בהנאה מועטת, כמו (שמות טו:ט) תמלאמו נפשי, לשון השגת תאוה; ואחרי שכן הוא — (ח) **מה יותר** לו בחכמתו משאם היה כסיל, **ומה־לעני** חסרון מן העשיר, שאין לו קורת רוח? גם הוא **יודע להלוך** בארץ **אצל החיים**. דבר אחר, **וגם־הנפש לא תמלא** לעולם הבא, שהרי לא עשה מעשים טובים בחייו: (ט) **טוב מראה עינים מהלך־נפש**. טוב היה והוכשר לזה לראות עושרו למראה עיניו ממאכל ומשתה ההולך בנפש. דבר אחר, **טוב מראה עינים מהלך־נפש** — טוב היה לזה והוכשר ללכת אחר עיניו לגזול ולעשוק מהילוך נפשו, שלא נתן לב היכן נפשו תלך כשימות: **גם־זה הבל**. הוא הניתן לרשעים: (י) **מה־שהיה כבר נקרא שמו**. חשיבות וגדולה שהיתה לו בחייו **כבר נקרא שמו**, כלומר, כבר היה ועבר, כבר יצא לו שם בשררה, ועתה חלף **ונודע שהוא אדם** ולא אל וסופו שמת **ולא־יוכל לדין עם** מלאך המות, **שהוא תקיף ממנו**:

7–12 / Greed — the source of unhappiness

7] FILLING HIS MOUTH . . . The man who has no higher values lives to eat and eats to live. But there is a natural limit to what a man can eat. Then why does he always have an appetite for more and more, even after he has attained enough to fill his mouth?

YET HIS APPETITE IS NOT SATED. The appetite, the lust for more and more, is the source of man's unhappiness. He could be content; he could be satisfied when he has enough to fill his mouth, but envy and illusions of ultimate happiness cause him to cast away opportunities for enjoyment today.

7] All man's labor is for the sake of filling his mouth — yet his appetite is not sated.

8] What advantage has the wise man over the fool; the one who knows how to cope with life over the destitute?

9] Better to experience hallucinations than to pursue desire — this, too, is vanity and chasing after wind.

10] What a man's lot shall be has already been determined and is known since his creation — and it is useless for him to contend with what is mightier than he.

8] WHAT ADVANTAGE HAS THE WISE MAN ... Even a wise man, an intelligent person, may be misled by his appetite to believe that he can find shortcuts to wealth so as not to spend all his days in the pursuit of money as the fool does. He may enter the contest to acquire possessions and believe that he will get more out of life than the fool. Alas, the appetite for money makes fools even of the wise. They usually end up kneeling before the golden calf.

9] BETTER ... HALLUCINATIONS ... Sometimes it is not envy that motivates the wise man. He may be misled by his hallucinations to believe that he can, with relatively little effort, realize his plans to acquire wealth. Koheleth warns that this too may have grievous results. Besides it does not avail man to plan and scheme, for he will in the end not acquire more than has been allotted to him.

10] HAS ALREADY BEEN DETERMINED ... Whether a man will be wealthy or not is determined by Elohim. Therefore,

יא] כִּי יֵשׁ־דְּבָרִים הַרְבֵּה מַרְבִּים הָבֶל מַה־יֹּתֵר לָאָדָם׃
יב] כִּי מִי־יוֹדֵעַ מַה־טּוֹב לָאָדָם בַּחַיִּים מִסְפַּר יְמֵי־חַיֵּי הֶבְלוֹ
וְיַעֲשֵׂם כַּצֵּל אֲשֶׁר מִי־יַגִּיד לָאָדָם מַה־יִּהְיֶה אַחֲרָיו תַּחַת
הַשָּׁמֶשׁ׃

(יא) **כי יש־דברים הרבה** שנתעסק בהן בחייו, כשחוק המלכים קופים ופילים ואריות — הכל [מה] הרבו לו (ע׳ קה״ר), ומה־יתר לו משמת ?! (יב) **כי מי־ידע.** כי מי אשר יודע מעשים טובים ומה־[טוב] **לאדם** לעשות בחייו, שיהיו טובים לו לעולם הארוך: **מספר ימי־חיי הבלו.** שהם מעט מספר, **ויעשם** לאותם מעשים בשעה מועטת שהוא חי, שהוא זמן קצר **כצל** עוף העובר; ואף על פי שאמר שלמה כצל סתם ולא פירש אם צל דקל אם צל כותל שהם קבועים, כבר פירשו דוד אביו (תהלים קמד: ד) ימיו כצל עובר, זהו צלו של עוף הפורח כך נדרש במדרש (ע׳ קה״ר); כי **מי־יגיד לאדם** במה יתקיים הון שקבץ מעושק לבניו **אחריו תחת השמש:**

says Koheleth, it is useless for man to dedicate his days and nights to the search for gain. He will acquire the same wealth whether he devotes three or thirteen hours a day to the project. The implication is that man would be wise if he were content with his share whatever it is and would devote time to the pursuit of higher values and to the performance of good deeds.

USELESS TO CONTEND WITH WHAT IS MIGHTIER . . . Man's innate greed, his desire to possess what another has, is his nemesis. Just as his share of wealth is determined, so is the other fellow's. It is useless for man to desire what Elohim has granted to another.

11] SO MANY THINGS . . . INCREASE VANITY . . . Men are tempted by many things that lead only to vanity. Those who have wealth want more. Even if they attain most of their material aims, they are not satisfied. Meanwhile they have lost much of the enjoyment of living. They have suffered

11] There are so many things that serve only to increase vanity. Why does man always seek more?

12] Who knows what is better for man in the vain life he spends as a shadow? Who can tell him what will be after him under the sun?

anxiety and vexation during the better part of a lifetime. Those who seek glory are equally unhappy, for they never have enough of it.

WHY DOES MAN ALWAYS SEEK MORE? At the root of materialistic man's failure to achieve happiness lies the insatiable desire for more. Man could be happy if he would be content. But he brings evil upon himself when he submits to the vanities — more money, more glory, more power.

12] WHO KNOWS WHAT IS BETTER . . . Those who consider themselves good friends have no right to urge a man on to seek more wealth and glory. For how do they know what is better for him, or how much he is destined to possess?

IN THE VAIN LIFE HE SPENDS AS A SHADOW . . . In the long span of human history, man's life is like a shadow, "now you see it and now you don't"; therefore, in his limited lifespan he should enjoy every moment. Life could be enjoyable if man counted his blessings each day.

WHO CAN TELL HIM . . . Nobody has the right to tell him, because nobody can know what the next day will bring or what will happen to a man's wealth after he is gone. Who can assure him that he will enjoy living once he enters the race for material gain? Who can guarantee him that his children will not squander his wealth?

Chapter 7

REPENTANCE

Let not the repentant suppose
that he is kept far away from the degree
attained by the righteous,
because of the iniquities and sins
that he has committed. This is not so.
He is beloved by the Creator,
desired by Him, as if he had never sinned.

Maimonides

א] טוֹב שֵׁם מִשֶּׁמֶן טוֹב וְיוֹם הַמָּוֶת מִיּוֹם הִוָּלְדוֹ׃

ב] טוֹב לָלֶכֶת אֶל־בֵּית־אֵבֶל מִלֶּכֶת אֶל־בֵּית מִשְׁתֶּה בַּאֲשֶׁר הוּא סוֹף כָּל־הָאָדָם וְהַחַי יִתֵּן אֶל־לִבּוֹ׃

(א) **טוב שם משמן טוב.** יפה לאדם שם טוב משמן טוב, **וביום המות** טוב השם **מיום הולדו.** לכך הוקש שם טוב לשמן יותר משאר משקין, שהשמן — אתה נותן לתוכו מים והוא צף ועולה וניכר, אבל שאר משקין — אתה נותן לתוכן מים והם בולעים; טוב שם משמן טוב, שמן טוב יורד למטה, שנאמר (תהלים קלג: ב) כשמן הטוב [על־הראש] ירד על־הזקן, שם טוב עולה למעלה, שנאמר (בראשית יב: ב) ואגדלה שמך. שמן טוב — לשעה, ושם טוב — לעולם, שנאמר (תהלים עב: יז) יהי שמו לעולם. שמן טוב הולך מקיתון לטרקלין ולא יותר. ושם טוב — לסוף העולם. אמר רבי יהודה ברבי סימון: מצינו בעלי שמן טוב נכנסו למקום החיים ויצאו שרופים, והם נדב ואביהוא שנמשחו בשמן המשחה, ומצינו בעלי שם טוב שנכנסו למקום המיתה ויצאו חיים — חנניה מישאל ועזריה שיצאו מכבשן האש: **ויום המות מיום הולדו.** נולדה מרים — אין הכל יודעין מה היא, מתה — נסתלקה הבאר; וכן אהרן בעמוד ענן, וכן משה במן (תנחומא ויקהל א): (ב) **טוב ללכת אל־בית־אבל.** מדה הנוהגת בחיים ובמתים: **מלכת אל־בית משתה.** שהיא מדה שאינה נוהגת אלא בחיים: **באשר הוא סוף כל־האדם.** בשביל שהאבל הוא סוף כל האדם, סופו של כל אדם לבא לידי כך; לפיכך **החי יתן אל־לבו.** כל מה שאגמול חסד עם המת, אצטרך אני שיגמלו לי במותי, דידל ידלוניה דיטען יטענוניה דיספד יספדוניה דיילוה ילויניה (כתובות עב ע״א). דבר אחר, **באשר הוא סוף כל־האדם.** שהמיתה היא סוף כל ימי האדם, ואם לא עכשיו גומל לו חסד לא יגמול לו עוד; אבל **בית המשתה** — זימנו ולא הלך יוכל לומר לו, סופך שיולד לך בן ושם אהיה עמך, תבא לך שמחת חתונת בניך ושם אלך; **והחי יתן אל־לבו.** הדבר הזה,

1–12 / Wisdom for the wise

1] Better a good name than precious oil . . . A good name comes as a result of much effort; it is the reward for a conscientious struggle against temptation and selfishness. Whatever the source of the good name — whether it comes

1] Better a good name than precious oil; and the day of death than the day of birth.

2] Better to go to a house of mourning than to a banquet hall, for that is the end of all men and the living will take it to heart.

as the result of one's devotion to family, or one's service to one's friends, or honesty in business dealings, or the practice of good deeds, or any combination of these — it is *earned*.

However, precious oil which is used to anoint kings merely bestows a title because of noble birth. The title is yet to be earned; we do not know what time will reveal about the nature of the king. Will he show great leadership and earn the title or will he indulge himself at the expense of his people?

Therefore, a good name is better, for it is earned; anointment signifies only an empty title, a claim to be proven.

AND THE DAY OF DEATH . . . Likewise, on the day of death a person has already earned his good name. But on the day of birth we do not know what will become of the infant during his lifetime. He has yet to prove himself.

2] BETTER TO GO TO A HOUSE OF MOURNING . . . If one is confronted with the choice, then better a house of mourning. The visit to a house of mourning immediately achieves two purposes: it suppresses the selfish desire to avoid the unpleasant; it is a source of comfort and consolation for a friend in sorrow. On the other hand, attendance at a banquet hall is merely fleeting physical pleasure and indulgence of the body.

ג] טוֹב כַּעַס מִשְּׂחוֹק כִּי־בְרֹעַ פָּנִים יִיטַב לֵב:
ד] לֵב חֲכָמִים בְּבֵית אֵבֶל וְלֵב כְּסִילִים בְּבֵית שִׂמְחָה:
ה] טוֹב לִשְׁמֹעַ גַּעֲרַת חָכָם מֵאִישׁ שֹׁמֵעַ שִׁיר כְּסִילִים:

שאם לא עכשיו יגמול לו חסד, לא יגמול לו עוד: **(ג) טוב כעס משחוק.** מי שרודפת מדת הדין אחריו, אל יצטער; טוב היה להם לדור המבול אם הראם הקדוש ברוך הוא פנים זעומות על עבירות שבידם משחוק ששחק עמהם, שאילו הראה להם קימעא רוע פנים היו חוזרים למוטב; טוב היה לאדוניהו אם עצבו אביו על כל עבירה שהיה עושה משחוק שהראה לו, ובסוף נהרג עליו (ע' קה"ר): **ייטב לב.** יהפוך לב האדם להטיב דרכיו: **(ד) לב חכמים בבית אבל.** מחשבתם על יום המיתה: **ולב כסילים בבית שמחה.** אין חרדים מיום

AND THE LIVING WILL TAKE IT TO HEART. Man must be occupied either in physical work or in mental reflection. As pointed out in the previous verse, one can acquire a good name only by work, physical or mental. One cannot achieve without effort. "Idleness breeds moral deterioration," say the Rabbis. The house of mourning serves as a source for reflection on life, its relatively short duration, and the need to make the most of each day. Thus, when one goes to a house of mourning, there is not only the virtue of the good deed but also the very important outcome of serious reflection. Attendance at a banquet hall, however, leads only to the questionable advantage of a full stomach and even to possible moral deterioration caused by flightiness.

3] BETTER AN ANGRY POSTURE . . . Koheleth most likely refers here to the apparent angry look and sad countenance that usually characterize a person in serious reflection. This outward appearance of anger is merely a surface expression caused by absorption in thought. Actual anger is despised by Koheleth (see verse 9, this chapter).

Reflection, even if it is masked by anger and sadness, will

3] Better an angry posture than light-heartedness, for a sad countenance leads to gladness in the heart.

4] Wise men's hearts are attracted to a house of mourning; the hearts of fools are attracted to a house of mirth.

5] Better to hear the reproof of the wise than for a man to hear the song of fools.

no doubt be of greater good than light-heartedness accompanied by empty-mindedness.

LEADS TO GLADNESS ... Reflection is only masked by a sad countenance. Meanwhile, the mind is occupied and desires are suppressed. Ultimately this gives one the satisfactory feeling of moral achievement which gladdens the heart.

4] WISE MEN'S HEARTS ... Wise men's hearts tend toward the serious reflection which is initiated in a house of mourning. The wise man will not permit himself to be dominated by his desires, by flighty thinking. He will prefer serious reflection.

The fool, on the other hand, is led by his desires; he makes little attempt to control them. His heart is dominated by the inanity of the house of mirth.

5] BETTER TO HEAR THE REPROOF OF THE WISE ... Often the criticism of the wise may be harsh and cruel but ultimately it helps to correct our errors and to set us aright. Whereas the song of fools — the fawning of sycophants, and the praise heaped upon us by fools — is usually insincere and serves only to confirm our faults and increase our arrogance.

ו] כִּי כְקוֹל הַסִּירִים תַּחַת הַסִּיר כֵּן שְׂחֹק הַכְּסִיל וְגַם־זֶה הָבֶל׃
ז] כִּי הָעֹשֶׁק יְהוֹלֵל חָכָם וִיאַבֵּד אֶת־לֵב מַתָּנָה׃
ח] טוֹב אַחֲרִית דָּבָר מֵרֵאשִׁיתוֹ טוֹב אֶרֶךְ־רוּחַ מִגְּבַהּ רוּחַ׃
ט] אַל־תְּבַהֵל בְּרוּחֲךָ לִכְעוֹס כִּי כַעַס בְּחֵיק כְּסִילִים יָנוּחַ׃

המיתה, ולבם בריא כאולם: **(ו) כי כקול הסירים** — עצי קוצים, אשפי״נש בלעז (**aspins, thorns**), **תחת הסיר**. תחת סיר נחשת הכפוי על תבערת קוצים והם מקשקשים לתוכה. אמר רבי יהושע בן לוי, כל קיסיא כד אינון דלקין — לית קלהון אזיל, ברם הלין סירייתא קלהון אזיל, למימר אף אנן מן קיסיא (קהלת זוטא; וע׳ קה״ר), מודיעים אף אנו מן העצים ויש צורך בנו, אף הכסילים מרבים דברים לומר גם אנו מן החשובים: **וגם־זה הבל** ועמל הוא, שמסר הקדוש ברוך הוא לבריות להיות יגעים, ומקנתרים בהם: **(ז) כי העשק יהולל חכם**. כשהכסיל מקנתר את החכם, מערבב דעתו וגם הוא נכשל (תנחומא וארא ה); דתן ואבירם קנתרו את משה לומר (שמות ה:כא) ירא ה׳ עליכם וישפט וגומר, וערבבוהו ואבדו את לבו וגרמו לו שהקפיד כנגד הקדוש ברוך הוא ואמר (שם ה:כג) והצל לא־הצלת את־עמך, ונענש בדבר שהשיבו (שם ו:א) עתה תראה — ולא תראה במלחמת שלשים ואחד מלכים (סנהדרין קיא ע״א, תנחומא ב׳ וארא אות ד): **לב מתנה**. לב חכמה שהיא מתנה לאדם, שנאמר (משלי ב:ו) כי־ה׳ יתן חכמה (תנחומא שם): **עושק**. לשון ריב וקנתורין: יש פנים אחרים, אך מפרידין המקראות זו מזו, ו־כי האמור בראש המקרא מוכיח שמחובר למקרא שלפניו: **(ח) טוב אחרית דבר מראשיתו**. כמשמעו, בראשית הדבר אין אנו יודעים מה יהא בסופו, אבל כשאחריתו טוב נגמר בטובה. דבר אחר, **טוב אחרית דבר מראשיתו** — בזמן שהוא מראשיתו טוב, שנתכוונו לטובה כשהתחילו בו; רבי מאיר הוי קאים ודריש כולה מילתא באלישע בן אבויה — במדרש קהלת (וע׳ ירושלמי חגיגה פ״ב ה״א): **ארך־רוח**. המאריך רוגזו ואינו ממהר לריב:

6] LIKE THE CRACKLING OF THORNS . . . Thorns aflame make a great deal of noise but produce little heat. So the laughter of the fool is noisy, but has very little in content to cheer us and still less to teach us.

7] THE PROVOCATIVENESS OF THE FOOL . . . The cackling of the fool is frequently upsetting and may provoke the wise man into a fit of emotion. The wise man thus becomes dis-

6] For like the crackling of thorns under the pot, so the laughter of the fool. And this, too, is vanity.

7] The provocativeness of the fool can disarm the wise man and can destroy his understanding.

8] Better a matter at its end than at its beginning; better patience than over-confidence.

9] Hasten not to rouse your spirits in anger, for anger rankles in the bosom of fools.

armed; the calm necessary for logical thinking and understanding is destroyed.

8] BETTER A MATTER AT ITS END . . . One should not hasten to reach conclusions about a new venture or new idea at its beginning. There are so many unforeseen circumstances involved in the actual implementation that it is generally prudent to suspend judgment until the end.

Likewise, patience is recommended in any worthwhile undertaking, rather than over-confidence, which is frequently blinding and misleading.

9] HASTEN NOT . . . IN ANGER . . . Man's greatest asset is his ability to moderate, even to subdue, his emotions — to think rationally. To the extent that an individual permits his emotions to control him, to that extent is he disarmed of clear thinking.

One of our most powerful emotions is anger — so powerful as to produce profound bodily changes. We are advised to train ourselves not to be carried away hastily in a fit of anger. Only the person who learns to face tension-filled situa-

י אַל־תֹּאמַר מֶה הָיָה שֶׁהַיָּמִים הָרִאשֹׁנִים הָיוּ טוֹבִים מֵאֵלֶּה
כִּי לֹא מֵחָכְמָה שָׁאַלְתָּ עַל־זֶה:
יא טוֹבָה חָכְמָה עִם־נַחֲלָה וְיֹתֵר לְרֹאֵי הַשָּׁמֶשׁ:

(ט) אל-תבהל. אל תמהר: **(י) אל-תאמר מה היה שהימים וגומר.** אל תתמה על הטובה שהיתה באה על הצדיקים הראשונים כדור המדבר ודורו של יהושע ודורו של דוד. **כי לא מחכמה שאלת.** שהכל לפי זכות הדורות: **(יא) טובה חכמה וגו'.** חכמתם עמדה להם עם נחלת זכות אבותם, כי טובה היא החכמה: **ויתר לראי השמש.** יתרון היא החכמה לכל הבריות: **ראי השמש** הן כל הבריות, כדתנן (נדרים פ"ג מ"ז) הנודר מרואי החמה אסור אף בסומין, לא

tions with calmness can avoid anger and the concomitant loss of rationality.

Challenging crises and frustrating experiences must be accepted as an integral part of living. Perhaps they are Elohim's way of trying us to see whether we can be masters of the situation or whether we will succumb to our emotions. There is no doubt that the only sane and profitable approach to an emotion-filled crisis is a reasoned study of the condition and its causes. If one submits to anger one loses the option to reason — one makes a fool of oneself.

10] Why were the former days better . . .? One of man's sources of happiness is his ability to face up to many of the challenges of living and to overcome them. Man has to have the feeling of mastery and achievement born of determination and persistent effort, especially in moral and spiritual situations.

Men who have failed because of lack of moral fortitude usually resort to excuses. One of the common rationalizations is "the former days were better," as if to say that it was easier to bring up children in former days, and so on. These

10] Do not say, "Why were the former days better than these?" For it is not wisdom that prompts you to ask this question.

11] It is good to have wisdom and an inheritance; it is considered a greater advantage by all who see the sun.

excuses are only defense mechanisms, balm to soothe a guilty conscience.

FOR IT IS NOT WISDOM . . . The question does not stem from an objective comparative study of past and present. It is rather a way out from a feeling of guilt for shirking responsibility in the present. It is an emotional response rather than a rational response.

Wisdom would have prompted the individual to face up to his problems and to master them.

11] IT IS GOOD TO HAVE WISDOM AND AN INHERITANCE . . . The ideal combination is the possession of wisdom and wealth. If wealth is to fall into someone's hands, it is better that it fall into the hands of a wise person. He will know how to best use and how to best preserve that wealth. This is not to say that Koheleth bestows upon wealth a value equal to wisdom. Throughout his writings, he stresses the superiority of wisdom even as he does in the following verse. It is rather the reaction of Koheleth to the destruction of wealth when it falls into the hands of fools, a fact that he tragically bemoans, in an earlier chapter (2:18,19).

יב) כִּי בְּצֵל הַחָכְמָה בְּצֵל הַכָּסֶף וְיִתְרוֹן דַּעַת הַחָכְמָה תְּחַיֶּה
בְעָלֶיהָ:

נתכוון זה אלא במי שהחמה רואה אותו: (יב) כי בצל החכמה בצל הכסף. כל מי שישנו בצל החכמה ישנו בצל הכסף, שהחכמה גורמת לעושר שיבא: ויתרון דעת החכמה תחיה בעליה. ועוד החכמה יתירה על הכסף, שהחכמה תחיה בעליה:

12] For wisdom protects . . . Here protection is used in the sense of security. The security of wisdom is as the security of money. People look to money as a source of security. But Koheleth assures us that wisdom is at least equally a source of security. In fact, a person of meager means but of superior wisdom and intelligence is surely more secure in facing the

12] For wisdom protects as well as money, and there is advantage in the knowledge that wisdom gives vibrancy to its possessor.

problems of life than is the individual who is wealthy but lacks wisdom.

THERE IS ADVANTAGE . . . The value of wisdom is greater because of its fundamental nature. Wisdom provides the color, interest and vigor to living that all the money in the world cannot buy.

יג] רְאֵה אֶת־מַעֲשֵׂה הָאֱלֹהִים כִּי מִי יוּכַל לְתַקֵּן אֵת אֲשֶׁר עִוְּתוֹ׃
יד] בְּיוֹם טוֹבָה הֱיֵה בְטוֹב וּבְיוֹם רָעָה רְאֵה גַּם אֶת־זֶה לְעֻמַּת־
זֶה עָשָׂה הָאֱלֹהִים עַל־דִּבְרַת שֶׁלֹּא יִמְצָא הָאָדָם אַחֲרָיו
מְאוּמָה׃

(יג) **ראה את־מעשה האלהים.** היאך הוא מתוקן, הכל לפי הפעולה של אדם — גן עדן לצדיקים וגיהנם לרשעים, ראה לך באיזה תדבק: **כי מי יוכל לתקן** לאחר מיתה **את הדבר אשר עותו** בחייו: (יד) **ביום טובה היה בטוב.** ביום שיש בידך לעשות טובה, היה בעושי הטובה: **וביום רעה ראה.** כשתבוא הרעה על הרשעים אתה תהיה מן הרואים, שנאמר (ישעיה סו:כד) ויצאו וראו בפגרי האנשים וגו׳, ולא תהיה מן הנראים — והיו דראון לכל־בשר: **גם את־זה לעמת־זה.** הטובה ושכר פעולתה לעמת הרעה ושכר פעולתה: **(אשר לא) [שלא]**

13–20 / Repentance — Elohim's special gift to man

13] Consider the deeds of Elohim . . . The greatest gift Elohim has granted to man is — repentance.

Elohim allows man absolute freedom of choice to perform good or evil. Man is, so to speak, put to the test — whether he will see Elohim in the universe, whether he will maintain his faith in spite of his witnessing much suffering and evil, whether he will rise above the pursuit of material gain to attain spiritual goals and perform good deeds. Logic would dictate that if man failed, he should be doomed. Yet Elohim extends to him, even when he is immersed in sin, the opportunity to repair what he has made crooked. He need but reflect and repent and he is given the opportunity to start all over again with a new slate.

14] On the day . . . rejoice. Good deeds bring inner satisfaction and happiness; they contain their own reward.

13] Consider the deeds of Elohim — else, how could one repair what he has made crooked?

14] On the day that you have performed good deeds — rejoice; and on the day that you have committed evil — reflect; for Elohim has set up one against the other, so that man could erase all and leave naught behind.

It is pleasant and comforting to know that one has set aside selfish interests in order to bring happpiness to others. Rejoicing in such thought encourages future performance of good deeds.

ON THE DAY . . . REFLECT. On the other hand, if one has committed evil, he need not despair. If he has compunctions, he should reflect on the fact that Elohim extends to him an opportunity to repent and start anew — no matter how far gone he might be. To sin and to callously ignore the fact is to cut one's lifeline. In such a case punishment in some form or other is inevitable. The only way to run away from Elohim is to run to Him.

ONE AGAINST THE OTHER . . . Repentance against sin.

MAN COULD ERASE ALL . . . In man's formidable struggle to elevate himself, in his failures and frustrations, there is always the encouraging thought that Elohim will accept him in spite of his imperfections. There is always hope; always another chance. Man knows that he could erase all guilt through repentance; that all his past sins will be forgiven and forgotten, if he rejects his past and starts afresh in all sincerity. He starts a new account and leaves no record or stain of sin behind.

טו] אֶת־הַכֹּל רָאִיתִי בִּימֵי הֶבְלִי יֵשׁ צַדִּיק אֹבֵד בְּצִדְקוֹ וְיֵשׁ
רָשָׁע מַאֲרִיךְ בְּרָעָתוֹ:
טז] אַל־תְּהִי צַדִּיק הַרְבֵּה וְאַל־תִּתְחַכַּם יוֹתֵר לָמָּה תִּשּׁוֹמֵם:
יז] אַל־תִּרְשַׁע הַרְבֵּה וְאַל־תְּהִי סָכָל לָמָּה תָמוּת בְּלֹא עִתֶּךָ:
יח] טוֹב אֲשֶׁר תֶּאֱחֹז בָּזֶה וְגַם־מִזֶּה אַל־תַּנַּח אֶת־יָדֶךָ כִּי־יְרֵא
אֱלֹהִים יֵצֵא אֶת־כֻּלָּם:

ימצא האדם אחריו מאומה. להרהר אחריו של הקדוש ברוך הוא: (טו) **יש צדיק אבד בצדקו.** אף על פי שהוא אובד, עודנו עומד בצדקו. מעשה ביוסף בן פנחס הכהן, שעלתה נומי ברגלו; קראו לרופא לחתוך רגלו; אמר לו, כשאתה מגיע לחוט השערה הודיעני, וכן עשה; קרא לחוניא בנו, אמר לו, בני, עד כאן היית חייב ליטפל בי, מכאן ואילך אין אתה חייב ליטפל בי, שאין כהן מיטמא לאבר מן החי מאביו (ע׳ ירושלמי נזיר פ״ז ה״א; תורת כהנים פ׳ אמור): (טז) **אל־תהי צדיק הרבה** — כשאול שדימה להיות צדיק וריחם על הרשעים, **ואל־תתחכם יותר.** לדון קל וחומר של שטות, ומה על נפש אחת אמרה תורה הבא עגלה ערופה וכו׳ (יומא כב ע״ב): (יז) **אל־תרשע הרבה.** אפילו רשעת מעט — אל תוסיף להרשיע, **למה תמות בלא עתך** — כשאול, שנאמר (דברי הימים א׳ י: יג) וימת שאול במעלו אשר־מעל [בה׳] — בנוב עיר הכהנים ובעמלק (ויקרא רבה פכ״ו ז): (יח) **טוב אשר תאחז בזה וגומר.** אחוז בצדק

15] A RIGHTEOUS MAN WHO PERISHES . . . One of the frustrations man faces, in his spiritual struggle in this world, is the paradox that sometimes the righteous suffer and perish at an early age, whereas the wicked enjoy worldly goods and endure. Yet man is asked not to lose faith in spite of this apparent incongruity. This is part of the trial, of the significant test he must undergo.

16] DO NOT BE OVER-RIGHTEOUS . . . The righteous sometimes go too far in their abstention from material goods — for example, by excessive fasting or punishment of the body. Elohim wants man to preserve a healthy body and to enjoy whatever material goods He has allotted him.

WHY DESTROY YOURSELF? Even to attain spiritual goals

15] I have seen everything in my vain days — even a righteous man who perishes in spite of his righteousness and a wicked man who endures despite his wickedness.

16] Do not be over-righteous nor too wise; why destroy yourself?

17] Do not indulge in evil. Don't be a fool. Why die before your time?

18] It is good to take a firm hold on the one, while at the same time not neglecting the other. For he who fears Elohim will do his duty by both.

one needs a healthy body. Weakness and sickness serve only to deprive man of the vigor he needs in his daily living and in his struggle for existence. To weaken the body is to destroy oneself materially and spiritually. Extreme spiritual living is inimical to normal health.

17] DON'T BE A FOOL. One who indulges in material extremes acts like a fool, for he permits himself to be ruled by passion and emotion rather than by reason.

WHY DIE BEFORE YOUR TIME? Excessive material enjoyments, gluttony and passion, violate all principles of physical and mental health and can only lead to self-destruction.

18] ON THE ONE . . . the spiritual.

WHILE NOT NEGLECTING THE OTHER . . . the material.

HE WHO FEARS ELOHIM WILL DO . . . BOTH. He who fears Elohim will do all he can to maintain a healthy body so that he will have the physical stamina to lead a vigorous and useful material and spiritual existence. He will partake of the spiritual and the material in moderation.

יט] הַחָכְמָה תָּעֹז לֶחָכָם מֵעֲשָׂרָה שַׁלִּיטִים אֲשֶׁר הָיוּ בָּעִיר:
כ] כִּי אָדָם אֵין צַדִּיק בָּאָרֶץ אֲשֶׁר יַעֲשֶׂה־טּוֹב וְלֹא יֶחֱטָא:

וברשע; אם אמר לך הנביא הצדיק דבר שהוא דומה לך לרשע, כגון שאמר שמואל לשאול — אל יקל בעיניך לפקפק בו: **יצא את־כלם** — ידי שניהם לקיים הצדק והרשע כהלכתן: (יט) **החכמה תעז לחכם.** לפי שאמר אל תרשע הרבה, אם רשעת מעט אל תוסף עליו, אלא פשפש במעשיך ותהא תוהא על החטא — אמר **החכמה תעז לחכם**, שהיא יועצתו לשוב בתשובה **מעשרה שליטים.** מצינו ביאשיהו, שהעיד עליו הכתוב (מלכים ב׳ כג: כה) וכמהו לא־היה לפניו מלך וגו׳ — הרי עמדה לו חכמתו שפשפש במעשיו, וטוב לו מעשרה מלכים שהרשיעו ולא שבו מדרכם **אשר היו בעיר**, בירושלים — רחבעם, אביה, אחזיה, יואש אחרי מות יהוידע, אמציה, אחז, מנשה, אמון, יהויקים, צדקיהו; (כ) **כי אדם אין צדיק בארץ.** לפיכך צריך לפשפש במעשיו:

19] Wisdom gives more strength . . . In order to face the incongruities of worldly existence one needs the fortitude provided by wisdom. Most life problems are solved only by wisdom. Even in situations where brute strength is helpful, the probability is that a better solution could be found through the utilization of wisdom.

19] Wisdom gives more strength to the wise man than ten rulers of the city.

20] For there is not a righteous man on earth who does only good and never sins.

20] For there is not a righteous man . . . Since no individual is sinless, and since sin may lead to despair, man may be tempted to give up hope of ever becoming righteous and therefore sink further into the grasp of his evil inclinations. What is needed most at this time is the strength and courage to reject the past and to begin anew with greater vigor to repent and to reconstruct oneself. This strength is gained from wisdom (verse 19).

כא) גַּם לְכָל־הַדְּבָרִים אֲשֶׁר יְדַבֵּרוּ אַל־תִּתֵּן לִבֶּךָ אֲשֶׁר לֹא־
תִשְׁמַע אֶת־עַבְדְּךָ מְקַלְלֶךָ׃
כב) כִּי גַּם־פְּעָמִים רַבּוֹת יָדַע לִבֶּךָ אֲשֶׁר גַּם־אַתָּ קִלַּלְתָּ אֲחֵרִים׃

(כא) גם לכל־הדברים וגומר. לפי שנדבר בשאול, שקיבל לשון הרע על נוב עיר הכהנים, ועליו נאמר אל תרשע הרבה, אמר **גם לכל־הדברים אשר ידברו** אליך הולכי רכיל **אל־תתן לבך** לקבלן, **אשר לא־תשמע את־עבדך** מקללך. אין טוב אשר תטה אזנך לשמוע את עבדך מקללך: דבר אחר (יט) **מעשרה שליטים.** אלו עשרה דברים המחייבים את האדם — שתי עיניו מראין אותו דבר עבירה; שתי אזניו משמיעין אותו דברים בטלים; שתי ידיו, שגוזל וחומס בהן; שתי רגליו, שמוליכין אותו לדבר עבירה; ופיו ולבו (ע׳ נדרים לב ע״ב): דבר אחר, החכמה תעוז לחכם — זה נח; מעשרה שליטים — מעשרה דורות שלפניו. דבר אחר, לחכם — זה יוסף; מעשרה שליטים — אלו אחיו. דבר אחר, לחכם — זה משה; מעשרה שליטים — עשרה דברים המשמשין את הגוף על ידי מאכל, מן פומא לוושטא, מן וושטא לכרסא וכו׳ כדאיתא במדרש קהלת, וחכמתו עמדה לו למשה, שלא נצטרך למאכל ארבעים יום וארבעים לילה. כל הפנים הללו במדרש (ע׳ קה״ר), ואיני יכול ליישב עליהן מקרא שלאחריו, כי אדם **אין צדיק בארץ:**

21–22 / Knowledge that does not bring happiness

21] DO NOT TAKE TO HEART EVERYTHING . . . Another way to maintain one's strength and one's mental health is to avoid being overly sensitive. Just as there is no person who has never sinned, so there is no person who has not been sinned against. Because of jealousies and prejudices there is no person who does not have enemies. One must not take these things

21] Also, do not take to heart everything that is spoken, lest you hear your own servant curse you.

22] For you know in your heart that you too have many times cursed others.

to heart so long as he knows that he has not willingly caused these reactions. It is a wicked streak in persons which awakens subconscious animosities to neighbors, even to friends. A man should not be surprised even if he should overhear his own servant curse him.

In order to maintain a happy frame of mind each person must learn, early in life, to discount unfounded animosities and the evil tongue.

22] YOU TOO HAVE . . . CURSED OTHERS. Even if you have not expressed the curse or animosity, you, too, have in your heart harbored such thoughts. Sometimes it is peculiar features or mannerisms, sometimes gaudy attire and sometimes the haughty aloofness of an individual that calls forth animosity or envy. Whatever the cause, it is experienced by every person to a greater or lesser degree. We must learn to control our own unwarranted envy or prejudiced animosity. But at the same time we must not be hypersensitive to it when we find it in others, as long as we have not knowingly initiated it.

כג) כָּל־זֹה נִסִּיתִי בַחָכְמָה אָמַרְתִּי אֶחְכָּמָה וְהִיא רְחוֹקָה מִמֶּנִּי׃
כד) רָחוֹק מַה־שֶּׁהָיָה וְעָמֹק עָמֹק מִי יִמְצָאֶנּוּ׃

(כג) כל־זה נסיתי בחכמה. מוסב על מקראות שלמטן (ועל שלמעלן): **נסיתי בחכמה.** בתורה: **אמרתי אחכמה.** לדעת את החכמה: **והיא רחוקה ממני.** ומה היא זו: **(כד) רחוק מה־שהיה,** את הדברים הרחוקים שהיו ביצירת בראשית: **ועמק עמק הוא מי ימצאנו** — שאין לי רשות להרהר בהן מה למעלה ומה למטה, מה לפנים ומה לאחור:

23–24 / Knowledge that is not attainable

23] All this I have probed . . . All these worldly matters, the importance of wisdom and its necessity for the attainment of happiness — all these have been tested by Koheleth in everyday living; he speaks from experience.

it was beyond me. There is, however, another kind of knowledge that I found could not be acquired by man. It is the

23] All this I have probed in regard to wisdom; I thought I could pursue wisdom even further but it was beyond me.

24] What has happened in the past is far beyond me and so profound as to defy discovery.

understanding of the nature of Elohim. I thought I could probe even further into His ways, but these are beyond the ability of the human mind, even the keenest of minds.

24] WHAT HAS HAPPENED IN THE PAST . . . How the world was created, how the spiritual was embodied in the material, what the conditions were before the world was created, the nature of time and space — all these are far beyond me. All these are so profound as to defy discovery by the limited human mind.

כה] סַבּוֹתִי אֲנִי וְלִבִּי לָדַעַת וְלָתוּר וּבַקֵּשׁ חָכְמָה וְחֶשְׁבּוֹן וְלָדַעַת
רֶשַׁע כֶּסֶל וְהַסִּכְלוּת הוֹלֵלוֹת:
כו] וּמוֹצֶא אֲנִי מַר מִמָּוֶת אֶת־הָאִשָּׁה אֲשֶׁר־הִיא מְצוֹדִים
וַחֲרָמִים לִבָּהּ אֲסוּרִים יָדֶיהָ טוֹב לִפְנֵי הָאֱלֹהִים יִמָּלֵט מִמֶּנָּה
וְחוֹטֵא יִלָּכֶד בָּהּ:
כז] רְאֵה זֶה מָצָאתִי אָמְרָה קֹהֶלֶת אַחַת לְאַחַת לִמְצֹא חֶשְׁבּוֹן:

(כה) **ועוד סבותי... לדעת ולתור ובקש חכמה** — פרשת פרה אדומה, **וחשבון** — קץ הגאולה, **ולדעת רשע כסל** — לעמוד על סוף דעתה של (מצותה) [אפיקורסות] **והסכלות הוללות** — מעורבב ומשועמם שבה: (כו) **ומוצא אני מר ממות**, שהיא קשה מעשרה דברים הקשים שנבראו בעולם, כדאיתא בהשותפין (בבא בתרא י ע״א); ומוצא אני מר וקשה ממנה **את־האשה** — זו המינות (ע׳ עבודה זרה יז ע״א עה״פ הרחק מעליה דרכך, משלי ה: ז): **וחרמים לבה.** לשון מכמורת, כמו (חבקוק א: טו) יגרהו בחרמו ויאספהו במכמרתו: **אסורים ידיה.** ומשהחזיקה באדם, הרי הוא כנקשר בקשורי עבותות: אסורים. שם דבר של קשורים, כמו (שופטים טו: יד) וימסו אסוריו — קשוריו; כן פירשו מנחם: (כז) **ראה זה מצאתי אמרה קהלת אחת לאחת למצא חשבון.** כל המצות שהצדיקים עושים והעבירות שהרשעים עוברים, נמנים לפני הקדוש ברוך הוא אחת על אחת עד שמצטרפות לחשבון גדול; כך פירשו רבותינו במסכת סוטה (ח ע״ב): **אמרה קהלת.** אמרה קבוצת החכמה, ואמרה נפשו המשכלת המקֻבצת החכמה: קהלת לשון נקבה היא, וכשהוא אומרו בלשון זכר — מוסב על הקבוצה, והוא שלמה (יב: ח, וע׳ רש״י שם). ובמדרש מצינו (קהלת זוטא) אמר רבי ירמיה בן אלעזר, [זה] רוח הקודש, פעמים משיחה בלשון זכר ופעמים משיחה בלשון נקבה, כתוב אחד אומר (תהלים ע: ו) עזרי

25–29 / One source of folly

25] I TURNED ABOUT AND APPLIED MY HEART ... After having found it futile for man to try to understand the motives of Elohim and His ways, Koheleth turns once more to apply himself directly to man, to his wisdom, to his wickedness and foolishness.

THE MOTIVATION OF THINGS ... What are the psychological motives behind man's behavior? What motivates the wisest

25] And so I turned about and applied my heart once more to know, to explore, to seek wisdom and the motivation of things, to know the nature of wickedness, foolishness, folly and madness.

26] And I find more bitter than death the woman whose heart is full of traps and snares, her hands as chains. He who seeks favor before Elohim will escape her, but the sinner will be trapped by her.

27] See, this I have found, says Koheleth, adding one thing to another to find an explanation.

of creatures to behave like the beast? Why does he seek outlets in foolishness, folly or madness? How can he direct his behavior to achieve happiness?

26] MORE BITTER THAN DEATH . . . One source of folly is man's indiscriminate, passionate involvement with woman. If passion dictates and wisdom is discarded, such an individual will fall into the hands of an unscrupulous woman and then life is more bitter than death.

THE WOMAN WHOSE HEART IS FULL OF TRAPS . . . Koheleth makes it clear that he speaks not of all women, but only of those who seek men for ulterior and selfish motives, and not out of love.

HER HANDS AS CHAINS . . . Once she has trapped the victim, she holds on to him with all tenacity. He is bound as if in chains.

27] SEE, THIS I HAVE FOUND . . . Man's failure to act wisely is almost always due to the fact that he allows his behavior

כח) אֲשֶׁר עוֹד־בִּקְשָׁה נַפְשִׁי וְלֹא מָצָאתִי אָדָם אֶחָד מֵאֶלֶף
מָצָאתִי וְאִשָּׁה בְכָל־אֵלֶּה לֹא מָצָאתִי:
כט) לְבַד רְאֵה־זֶה מָצָאתִי אֲשֶׁר עָשָׂה הָאֱלֹהִים אֶת־הָאָדָם יָשָׁר
וְהֵמָּה בִקְשׁוּ חִשְּׁבֹנוֹת רַבִּים:

ומפלטי, וכתוב אחד אומר (שם מ: יח) עזרתי ומפלטי; כתוב אחד אומר (ישעיה נב: ז) מה־נאוו על־ההרים רגלי מבשר, וכתוב אחד אומר (שם מ: ט) עלי־לך מבשרת ציון: (כח) **אשר עוד־בקשה נפשי.** לבד אלה האמורים למעלה, שבקשתים ולא מצאתים, בקשה עוד נפשי כשרה בנשים **ולא מצאתי,** כי כולן דעתן קלה עליהן: **אדם אחד מאלף מצאתי.** בנוהג שבעולם, אלף נכנסים למקרא — אין יוצאים מהם להצליח שראויים למשנה אלא מאה, ואותם מאה שנכנסו למשנה — אין יוצאים מהם לתלמוד אלא עשרה, ואותן עשרה שנכנסין לתלמוד — אין מצליח מהם אלא אחד [להוראה], הרי אחד מאלף (ויקרא רבה פ״ב א, וע׳ קה״ר). **ואשה בכל־אלה** — אפילו באלף; לכך אתה צריך להזהר בה: (כט) **לבד ראה־זה מצאתי.** שבאה לעולם תקלה על ידה: **אשר עשה** הקדוש ברוך הוא **את־האדם** הראשון **ישר, והמה,** משנזדווגה לו חוה אשתו ונעשו שנים ונקראו המה, **בקשו חשבנות רבים.** מזימות ומחשבות של חטא — כך נדרש במדרש (ע׳ קה״ר):

to be dictated by passion or emotion rather than by wisdom. Most of man's errors are committed by him under the influence of passion or emotion. One source of such folly is woman. The unscrupulous woman will permit, even encourage, man to continue his irrational behavior.

28] However, i have not found an explanation . . . Koheleth was disappointed by the fact that the upright man was rarely found and that the upright woman was almost nonexsistent. He could not explain why there was a difference between man and woman, in his time. One cannot imagine that he refers here to an actual statistical survey, but in his experience an upright man was rare (one in a thousand, perhaps) and an upright woman was even less frequently found.

28] However, I have not found an explanation for another phenomenon: why there should be one upright man in a thousand and why there should not be one upright woman among as many.

29] See, this much I have established: Elohim made man upright, but they have sought out many devices.

This is not a wholesale condemnation of women, as some have claimed. Koheleth (Solomon) was not particularly known to despise women. In Chapter 9 (verse 9) he says, "Enjoy life with the wife whom you love" and in Proverbs 18 (verse 22), "He who has found a woman has found the greatest good." He was simply puzzled by the fact that the "woman of valor" was so rare in his time.

ONE UPRIGHT MAN IN A THOUSAND ... The kind of man Koheleth seeks: one who counts his blessings each day, one who looks to perform good deeds, one who accepts his suffering graciously, one who is not a slave to material gain — such a man is indeed one in a thousand.

29] ELOHIM MADE MAN UPRIGHT ... Koheleth uses the word "man" here in the sense of the whole human race. Man and woman were created upright by Elohim. They could be guided, if they so willed it, by Elohim's commandments; they could live rationally and not be misled by their passions and emotions. But they have sought out many devices; they have formulated schemes to avoid rational control. They have permitted their animal instincts to dictate their behavior and to lead them astray.

Chapter 8

FAITH

And the righteous man
shall live by his faith.

Habakkuk

א] מִי כְּהֶחָכָם וּמִי יוֹדֵעַ פֵּשֶׁר דָּבָר חָכְמַת אָדָם תָּאִיר פָּנָיו וְעֹז
פָּנָיו יְשֻׁנֶּא:
ב] אֲנִי פִּי־מֶלֶךְ שְׁמֹר וְעַל דִּבְרַת שְׁבוּעַת אֱלֹהִים:

(א) **מי כהחכם.** מי בעולם כאדם חכם, **ומי יודע פשר דבר.** פשרון של דבר, כמו שמצינו בדניאל, מתוך חכמתו שהיה חכם ביראת שמים נתגלו לו רזי פשרין. מי כמשה עושה פשרים בין ישראל לאביהם שבשמים, **ועז פניו ישנא** משאר הבריות, עד כי (שמות לד: ל) יראו מגשת אליו כי קרן עור פניו (ע׳ קה״ר, קה״ז): (ב) **אני פי־מלך שמר.** לפיכך אני צריך ונכון לשמור פי מלכו של עולם, שהיא הטובה שבכולן, **ועל דברת שבועת אלהים** שנשבענו לו בחורב

1–4 / The wise man approaches Elohim

1] WHO CAN BE COMPARED TO THE WISE MAN . . . Over and over again, as in Proverbs so in Ecclesiastes, Solomon lauds the virtues of wisdom. Only wisdom truly liberates man to delight in contemplation, in the joyful mansions of thought.

WHO KNOWS THE INTERPRETATION OF THINGS. The wise man sees in natural phenomena and in life's problems challenges to thought and to interpretation. The wise man seeks to understand the universe. He is not content with a naturalistic explanation which depicts the universe as a self-manufacturing automaton.

The sun, the winds and the seas are not boring, repetitive phenomena. They have been created by Elohim to serve mankind. They are the voice of Elohim in nature calling to man to recognize His glories. The human body, the human mind, the animal and plant world are all subjects for contemplation and interpretation. There is so much in the universe to challenge the wise man that he can spend a lifetime in enjoyable meditation.

1] Who can be compared to the wise man and who knows the interpretation of things? A man's wisdom causes his face to shine, and the hardness of his features is changed.

2] I counsel you: observe the King's command; all the more because you have sworn allegiance to Elohim.

A MAN'S WISDOM CAUSES HIS FACE TO SHINE ... A man's wisdom permits him to enjoy reflection in his solitary moments; he can raise himself above his immediate environment even in the most trying circumstances. Gloom frequently disappears and the wise man is cheered when he realizes that he has the ability to meditate on life and its meaning and to find the interpretation of natural phenomena.

THE HARDNESS OF HIS FEATURES IS CHANGED. People who are not guided by wisdom are usually perplexed and frustrated by life's problems and responsibilities. Their disappointment is reflected in the hardening of their facial features. Even a potentially wise man who becomes a slave to wealth, to the planning and scheming for material gain, will take on the hard outer appearance that so often characterizes the wealthy tycoon.

But one who seeks greater values than the material will be possessed of cheer and optimism in the contemplation of these values. His outer features will reflect his inner contentment and happiness.

2] I COUNSEL YOU: OBSERVE THE KING'S COMMAND ... Koheleth realizes that to ask man to avoid jealousies, anger,

ג) אַל־תִּבָּהֵל מִפָּנָיו תֵּלֵךְ אַל־תַּעֲמֹד בְּדָבָר רָע כִּי כָּל־אֲשֶׁר
יַחְפֹּץ יַעֲשֶׂה׃
ד) בַּאֲשֶׁר דְּבַר־מֶלֶךְ שִׁלְטוֹן וּמִי יֹאמַר־לוֹ מַה־תַּעֲשֶׂה׃

לשמור מצוותיו. דבר אחר, אני נכון לשמור פי מלכי האומות המושלים בנו בגולגליות וארנוניות, ועל דברת שבועת אלהים — ובלבד שלא יעבירונו את השבועה שנשבענו למקום; ועל דברת — ואצל דברת שבועת אלהים אשמור פי המלכים; כן מצינו בחנניה, מישאל ועזריה, שאמרו לנבוכדנצר (דניאל ג:טז) ואמרין למלכא נבוכדנצר לא־חשחין אנחנא על־(דנא) [דנה] פתגם להתבותך, אם מלכא למה נבוכדנצר? ואם נבוכדנצר למה מלכא? אלא כך אמרו לו, לך אנו אומרים דאת מלכא לנו לעבודה ולמסים ולגולגליות, אך על דנא שאת אומר עלנא לעבוד עבודה זרה — נבוכדנצר את ולא מלך, ואת וכלבא שוין (ויקרא רבה פ׳ ל״ג ו; תנחומא נח י): (ג) **אל־תבהל מפניו תלך.** אל תהי נבהל לומר שתלך ותברח מפניו למקום שאינו שליט שם, שבכל מקום הוא שליט: **אל־תעמד בדבר רע.** אל תעמיד עצמך עוסק בדברים רעים, **כי כל־אשר יחפץ** להפרע ממך — רשות ויכולת בידו לעשות: (ד) **באשר דבר־מלך שלטון.** בשביל אשר דבר הקב״ה מושל הוא, **ומי יאמר־לו מה־תעשה?**

passion and the evil tongue merely on a rational basis is to ask him to perform the almost impossible. Man, even the wise man, tends to allow himself to succumb to his emotions. However, if man will look upon the control of his emotions as a command of the King of the universe then he will be strengthened in his convictions and in his ability to withstand temptation.

YOU HAVE SWORN ALLEGIANCE TO ELOHIM. The ancient Hebrew tradition, mentioned in the Talmud, has it that every child in his mother's womb, before birth, is pledged to be "righteous and not to be wicked." Though the final decision will always rest with each individual whether to do the righteous or the wicked, the good or the evil, it helps to know that the King is on your side when you resist evil. Passion and emotion are so powerful that each individual needs to possess the knowledge of the King's command and of his own

3] Do not attempt to hasten away from Him; do not persist in doing evil; He is omnipotent.
4] For the King's word is power; who can tell Him what to do?

pledge to righteousness in order to build up the moral fortitude required to overcome temptation.

3] DO NOT ATTEMPT TO HASTEN AWAY FROM HIM . . . Do not follow the infantile impulse to hasten out of the King's sight for He is omnipotent and omnipresent. If you have committed evil, reflect (7:14). You still have a chance to absolve yourself through repentance.

DO NOT PERSIST IN DOING EVIL . . . Repentance is effective only when one repents sincerely and actually breaks with the past. However, if one says, "I'll sin today and repent tomorrow," he is actually persisting in evil. He will not escape the purview of Elohim; he will not deceive Him. He is omnipotent. The only way to run away from Elohim (His judgment) is to run to Him (His mercy) in all sincerity.

4] FOR THE KING'S WORD IS POWER . . . Elohim's commands are not mere words or suggestions but compulsory prescriptions backed up by the power to punish those who defy, unless they should repent.

WHO CAN TELL HIM WHAT TO DO? To try to run away from Elohim is to imply that He is not omnipresent; to persist in evil is to imply that He is not omniscient. Both these attitudes reflect negatively on His omnipotence. He who persists in evil implies that he knows better than Elohim what to do or whether punishment should be meted out for his transgressions.

ה) שׁוֹמֵר מִצְוָה לֹא יֵדַע דָּבָר רָע וְעֵת וּמִשְׁפָּט יֵדַע לֵב חָכָם׃
ו) כִּי לְכָל־חֵפֶץ יֵשׁ עֵת וּמִשְׁפָּט כִּי־רָעַת הָאָדָם רַבָּה עָלָיו׃
ז) כִּי־אֵינֶנּוּ יֹדֵעַ מַה־שֶּׁיִּהְיֶה כִּי כַּאֲשֶׁר יִהְיֶה מִי יַגִּיד לוֹ׃
ח) אֵין אָדָם שַׁלִּיט בָּרוּחַ לִכְלוֹא אֶת־הָרוּחַ וְאֵין שִׁלְטוֹן בְּיוֹם
הַמָּוֶת וְאֵין מִשְׁלַחַת בַּמִּלְחָמָה וְלֹא־יְמַלֵּט רֶשַׁע אֶת־בְּעָלָיו׃

(ה) ואם שומר מצוה אתה — **לא תדע דבר רע** ולא תבואך: **ועת משפט ידע לב חכם.** החכם יודע שיש עת קבוע לפקודת רשעים ומשפט יש לפני הקדוש ברוך הוא, שסופו להפרע מהם. משפט יוסטי״צא בלעז (*justiça*, justice), והיא הפורענות: (ו) **כי לכל־חפץ,** שהאדם עושה חפצו ועובר על דת, **יש עת** להפרע, **ומשפט** ופורענות מוכנת: **כי־רעת האדם רבה עליו.** כאשר רבה רעת האדם וסאתו גדושה אז באה פקודתו. כי משמש בלשון כאשר, כמו (שמות יח: טז) כי־יהיה להם דבר בא אלי: (ז) **כי־איננו ידע מה־שיהיה.** כשהרשע עובר עבירה איננו נותן לבו למה שעתיד הקדוש ברוך הוא להביאו במשפט; ואוי לו בכך, **כי כאשר** יהיה הפורענות, **מי יגיד לו** להמלך בו וליטול בו עצה וליטול רשות, כי פתע פתאום יבואנו: (ח) **אין אדם שליט ברוח** — ברוחו ויצרו של שלוחו של מקום, **לכלוא** ולמנוע ממנו **את־הרוח** שבגופו, שלא יטלנו מלאך המות, **ואין שלטון** של שום מלך ניכר **ביום מותו**; בכל מקום אתה מוצא והמלך דוד, וביום מותו (מלכים א׳ ב: א) ויקרבו ימי־דוד למות, לא הוזכר מלכות כאן; **ואין משלחת במלחמה** זו לאמר, אשלח בני או עבדי

5-13 / Justice is inevitable

5] He who abides . . . will know no evil . . . Koheleth does not say that he who abides by His commands will *experience* no evil, for evil and good are everybody's lot in this world. However, the man who recognizes Elohim in the universe looks upon evil as necessary to provide man with choice and with ultimate reward; to test man's loyalty; to warn man to improve his ways (3:10). Such an approach to evil alleviates frustration and despair, and even encourages man to accept evil graciously.

The wise man knows in his heart . . . Though he is witness, at times, to the suffering of the righteous and the prospering

5] He who abides by His commands will know no evil; and the wise man knows in his heart that there will be a time of reckoning.

6] There is a time of reckoning for everything — the evil of man being so widespread.

7] For he does not know what to expect, and who can tell him when it will come.

8] But just as man has no power over the wind to stop the wind; just as he has no power over the day of death; just as he has no control over war — just as certainly will wickedness not help him to escape the inevitable punishment.

of the wicked, the wise man is convinced that ultimately justice will prevail.

6] THE EVIL OF MAN BEING SO WIDESPREAD. The oppression of man by his fellow-man being so widespread and being so characteristic of peoples and nations in all places and in all times, it is inevitable that Elohim will exact retribution from the oppressors, be they individuals or nations.

7] FOR HE [MAN] DOES NOT KNOW . . . The unfaithful do not immediately suffer and therefore do not believe in or expect ultimate punishment. There is no one who can tell them exactly when it will come.

8] BUT . . . But Koheleth is convinced through reason and experience that punishment will come during man's lifetime or immediately after death.

WILL WICKEDNESS NOT HELP . . . The more intelligent among the wicked try to rationalize their wickedness through a "sur-

ט] אֶת־כָּל־זֶה רָאִיתִי וְנָתוֹן אֶת־לִבִּי לְכָל־מַעֲשֶׂה אֲשֶׁר נַעֲשָׂה
תַּחַת הַשָּׁמֶשׁ עֵת אֲשֶׁר שָׁלַט הָאָדָם בְּאָדָם לְרַע לוֹ:
י] וּבְכֵן רָאִיתִי רְשָׁעִים קְבֻרִים וָבָאוּ וּמִמְּקוֹם קָדוֹשׁ יְהַלֵּכוּ
וְיִשְׁתַּכְּחוּ בָעִיר אֲשֶׁר כֵּן־עָשׂוּ גַּם־זֶה הָבֶל:
יא] אֲשֶׁר אֵין־נַעֲשָׂה פִתְגָם מַעֲשֵׂה הָרָעָה מְהֵרָה עַל־כֵּן מָלֵא
לֵב בְּנֵי־הָאָדָם בָּהֶם לַעֲשׂוֹת רָע:

במקומי (ע׳ קה״ר): (ט) **את־כל־זה** האמור למעלה, **ראיתי, ונתון את־לבי לכל־מעשה.** וגם לכל מעשה בני אדם נתתי את לבי וראיתי עת אשר שלט אדם בחבירו וגבר עליו וסופו נהפך לרעתו; עמלק נתגבר על ישראל וסופו (במדבר כד: כ) ואחריתו עדי אבד; כך פרעה, כן נבוכדנצר, וכן סנחריב: (י) **ובכן,** ואז, **ראיתי רשעים קברים.** בנבואה זו ראיתי רשעים קבורים, שהיו ראויים להטמן בעפר, שהיו נבזים בין שאר אומות, שנאמר עליהם (ישעיה כג: יג) זה העם לא היה (ע׳ ויק״ר פי״ז ד, סוכה נב ע״ב), ושלטו בביתו של הקדוש ברוך הוא שהוא מקום קדוש, ובלכתם משם אל ארצם היו משתבחים בעירם, אשר כך וכך עשו בביתו של מקום — אל תקרי וישתכחו, אלא וישתבחו; כך דרשוהו רבותינו זכרונם לברכה (גיטין נו ע״ב). ולענין השכחה כך נדרש באגדה (ע׳ קה״ר) וסופו שישתכח שמם וזכרם מן העיר עצמה אשר כן עשו בה, שנאמר (יואל ד: ב) וקבצתי את־כל־הגוים [והורדתים] אל־עמק יהושפט — במקום שניאצו לפניו יפרע מהם; וכן הוא אומר (תהלים עג: כ) ה׳ בעיר צלמם תבזה: **גם־זה** אחד מן ההבלים שנמסרו לעולם לייגע את הבריות, שאין הקדוש ברוך הוא ממהר להפרע בעושי הרעה, והבריות סבורים אין דין ואין דיין: (יא) **אשר אין־נעשה פתגם** — משפט — **מעשה הרעה מהרה.** שאין הקדוש ברוך הוא ממהר להפרע מעושי הרעה, ועל כן הם סבורים אין דין, ומלא לבם

vival of the fittest'' philosophy: the world is for the strong. But in the eyes of Elohim there is no justification for oppression and no amount of dialectic will help the oppressor to escape his punishment.

9] WHEN MEN EXERT POWER OVER THEIR FELLOW MEN . . . Just as between man and Elohim there is no escape from punishment, so between man and man no person or group can cause suffering to another person or group and escape with impunity.

9] All this I have seen as I applied my heart to all that takes place under the sun, especially when men exert power over their fellow men to hurt them.

10] And I have seen wicked persons buried and come forth whereas the righteous, whose source was holiness, go; consequently, they are forgotten in the very city where they performed righteousness. This, too, is vanity.

11] Because the sentence against him who performs the evil deed is not speedily executed, the hearts of men are encouraged to do evil.

10] WICKED PERSONS BURIED AND COME FORTH ... It is admittedly disappointing to see the wicked have offspring (interpreting "come forth" as referring to their offspring rather than to the wicked themselves) and prosper. But Koheleth is convinced that ultimately justice will prevail (verse 8).

THIS TOO IS VANITY. The fact, as mentioned above (verse 7), that no one can predict exactly when the evil-doer will be punished, and the fact that the evil-doer sometimes prospers and has offspring while a righteous man, at the same time and in the same city, may not prosper and may not have offspring, all add up to apparent injustice and disappointment. Man's attempts to understand these things are futile.

11] THE SENTENCE ... IS NOT SPEEDILY EXECUTED ... Because the evil-doer may go without punishment for a long time, he is encouraged to continue in his evil ways.

יב] אֲשֶׁר חֹטֶא עֹשֶׂה רָע מְאַת וּמַאֲרִיךְ לוֹ כִּי גַּם־יוֹדֵעַ אָנִי אֲשֶׁר
יִהְיֶה־טּוֹב לְיִרְאֵי הָאֱלֹהִים אֲשֶׁר יִירְאוּ מִלְּפָנָיו:
יג] וְטוֹב לֹא־יִהְיֶה לָרָשָׁע וְלֹא־יַאֲרִיךְ יָמִים כַּצֵּל אֲשֶׁר אֵינֶנּוּ
יָרֵא מִלִּפְנֵי אֱלֹהִים:

בקרבם לעשות רע: (יב) **אשר חטא וגו׳.** לפי שרואים שהחוטא **עושה רע מאת,** אלפים וריבואות, **ומאריך** לו הקדוש ברוך הוא ואינו נפרע ממנו: **מאת.** מקרא קצר ודבוק לפניו, לומר מאת ימים, מאת שנים, מאת אלף; וכן (ישעיה נא: כא) ושכרת, מקרא קצר וחסר — שכורת כעס ולא מיין כשאר שכרות: **כי גם־יודע אני.** כי אף בכל זאת, שאינו ממהר להפרע מן הרשעים ולהיות הפרש בין צדיקים לרשעים, יודע אני שסוף כל אחד ואחד ליטול שכרו, וליראיו יהיה טוב: (יג) **וטוב לא־יהיה לרשע,** לפי אשר איננו ירא מלפני (ה)אלהים:

12] I KNOW IT WILL BE GOOD . . . Koheleth is not shaken by the apparent injustice in the world. It is disappointing to the

12] A sinner may perform evil a hundred times over and Elohim is patient with him. I know it will be good with those who fear Elohim.

13] And it will not be well with the wicked man who does not fear Elohim. Like a shadow he will not long endure.

average man, but the man of faith is convinced of ultimate reward and punishment. He sees the paradox merely as a means of testing the loyalty of the righteous.

יד] יֵשׁ־הֶבֶל אֲשֶׁר נַעֲשָׂה עַל־הָאָרֶץ אֲשֶׁר יֵשׁ צַדִּיקִים אֲשֶׁר
מַגִּיעַ אֲלֵהֶם כְּמַעֲשֵׂה הָרְשָׁעִים וְיֵשׁ רְשָׁעִים שֶׁמַּגִּיעַ אֲלֵהֶם
כְּמַעֲשֵׂה הַצַּדִּיקִים אָמַרְתִּי שֶׁגַּם־זֶה הָבֶל:
טו] וְשִׁבַּחְתִּי אֲנִי אֶת־הַשִּׂמְחָה אֲשֶׁר אֵין־טוֹב לָאָדָם תַּחַת הַשֶּׁמֶשׁ
כִּי אִם־לֶאֱכֹל וְלִשְׁתּוֹת וְלִשְׂמוֹחַ וְהוּא יִלְוֶנּוּ בַעֲמָלוֹ יְמֵי חַיָּיו
אֲשֶׁר־נָתַן־לוֹ הָאֱלֹהִים תַּחַת הַשָּׁמֶשׁ:

(יד) **יש־הבל.** דבר המהביל את הבריות, **אשר יש צדיקים שמגיע אלהם** רעה **כמעשה הרשעים, ויש רשעים** שמגיע אלהם טובה **כמעשה הצדיקים, אמרתי** שגם זה אחד מן ההבלים הנוהגים בעולם. ורבותינו דרשו לצד אחר במסכת הוריות (י ע״ב), ואינו מיושב לי על שיטת דיבור שסיים החכם לומר שגם זה הבל: (טו) **את־השמחה.** שיהא שמח בחלקו ועוסק בפקודים ישרים משמחי לב, ולא יהא שטוף אחר הרבות הון בנשך ומרבית וגזל; כל מי שאינו שמח בחלקו ושטוף אחר הממון בא לידי עבירות, גזל ואונאה ורבית, ושאינו שמח בחלקו לענין אהבת אשתו שטוף אחרי הנשים להרהר אחרי אשת איש: **לאכול ולשתות** ממה שחנן לו הקדוש ברוך הוא **ולשמוח** בחלקו. ומדרש אגדה (ע׳ קה״ר), כל אכילה ושתיה שבקהלת אינה אלא תלמוד תורה, כענין שנאמר (ישעיה נה: א) לכו שברו ואכלו וגומר: **והוא** ילונו. יתחבר עמו, כענין שנאמר (שם נח: ח) והלך לפניו צדקך: **ימי חייו אשר־נתן־לו האלהים** יעשה כך; וסוף המקרא מוסב על ראשו ומקרא מסורס הוא — אין טוב לאדם ימי חייו אשר נתן

14–17 / Faith in spite of anomalies

14] RIGHTEOUS MEN WHO SUFFER . . . Here Koheleth spells out in all clarity the problem that irks man, even the wise and righteous man. It is anomalous for Elohim, who has in His providence created the universe and man, and contributed so much good to man, to allow the righteous to suffer and the wicked to prosper. Philosophically, the condition may be accepted as a test and challenge for man; it may be accepted as necessary in order to give man freedom of choice (3:10). But to most individuals it appears to be an anomaly that defies understanding.

14] There is a vanity that takes place on earth; there are righteous men who suffer as would befit those who perform wicked deeds, and there are wicked men who prosper as would befit those who perform good deeds. I say that this, too, is vanity.

15] Therefore, I commended joy, for there is no better thing under the sun than for man to eat, drink and be joyful, and this will accompany him in his toil all the days of his life that Elohim has granted him under the sun.

15] THERE IS NO BETTER THING . . . THAN FOR MAN TO EAT . . . In his limited lifetime and with his limited mind, it is futile for man to try to find the explanation for all these manifestations of evil. Man must assume that Elohim, whose hand is discernible in so much that is orderly and good in the universe, has created evil as part of His eternal plan. This evil is necessary for His purposes and must ultimately lead to good. However, it is futile for man to try to understand it.

This is what is meant by faith — faith in spite of anomalies. The man of faith is at peace with the world. He is grateful for all the good; and he accepts the evil gracefully, confident that it, too, is ultimately for the good. Only a man of such faith can eat, drink and be truly joyful.

As a man of faith he counts his blessings; he is contented with what he possesses and therefore enjoys his bread and his daily work.

THIS WILL ACCOMPANY HIM . . . ALL THE DAYS OF HIS LIFE . . . The individual who has trained himself to place his faith in

טז) כַּאֲשֶׁר נָתַתִּי אֶת־לִבִּי לָדַעַת חָכְמָה וְלִרְאוֹת אֶת־הָעִנְיָן
אֲשֶׁר נַעֲשָׂה עַל־הָאָרֶץ כִּי גַם בַּיּוֹם וּבַלַּיְלָה שֵׁנָה בְּעֵינָיו
אֵינֶנּוּ רֹאֶה׃
יז) וְרָאִיתִי אֶת־כָּל־מַעֲשֵׂה הָאֱלֹהִים כִּי לֹא יוּכַל הָאָדָם
לִמְצוֹא אֶת־הַמַּעֲשֶׂה אֲשֶׁר נַעֲשָׂה תַחַת־הַשֶּׁמֶשׁ בְּשֶׁל אֲשֶׁר
יַעֲמֹל הָאָדָם לְבַקֵּשׁ וְלֹא יִמְצָא וְגַם אִם־יֹאמַר הֶחָכָם לָדַעַת
לֹא יוּכַל לִמְצֹא׃

לו האלהים כי אם לאכול ולשתות ולשמוח, והוא ילונו בעמלו: (טז) **כאשר נתתי את־לבי.** אין כאשר זה משמש לשון דוגמא כמו כאשר עשה כן יעשה, אלא לשון זמן, כמו (בראשית לז:כג) כאשר־בא יוסף, (שם מג:ב) כאשר כלו לאכל; אף זה כן, כשהייתי נותן לבי לדעת (ולתור) [חכמה] וגומר, אז — וראיתי את כל מעשה האלהים: **שנה בעיניו איננו ראה.** הרשע השטוף אחר הממון והעריות: (יז) **וראיתי את־כל־מעשה האלהים** שמסר לבריות **כי לא יוכל האדם למצוא וגומר.** אין הבריות יכולין לעמוד על סוף דרכו של הקדוש ברוך הוא מה שכר כל המעשה שנעשה תחת השמש, שרואין רשעים מצליחים וצדיקים יורדים: **בשל אשר יעמל האדם לבקש.** בשביל אשר ראיתי הרבה עמלים לבקש ולמצוא את סוף המידה ואינן יכולין: **וגם אם־יאמר החכם** שהוא יודע — **לא יוכל,** שהרי משה רבינו לא עמד על הדבר, באומרו (שמות לג:יג) הודעני נא את־דרכך:

Elohim, to rejoice with what he has, will have developed the frame of mind that will make all his days happy ones.

16] FOR HE SLEEPS NEITHER BY DAY NOR BY NIGHT . . . Elohim is unceasingly at work on earth. His deeds are unlimited in number and their nature intricate and complex.

16] When I applied my heart to know wisdom and to perceive all that takes place on earth — for He sleeps neither by day nor by night —
17] when I viewed all the deeds of Elohim, I realized that man could not comprehend His ways under the sun; if the ordinary man will seek to fathom them, he will not succeed. And if the wise man should think that he could know them, he, too, will be at a loss.

17] THE WISE MAN . . . TOO WILL BE AT A LOSS. Man is able to discover the existence of Elohim, but he cannot fathom the ways of Elohim. The universe and all our surroundings point directly to a Creator Who made heaven and earth, the world of life, and the conditions for life. And yet there is much of evil, inequality, and even injustice. The human mind cannot explain all of the negative phenomena. The human being can only obey the commandments of Elohim and trust that the time will come when Elohim will reveal Himself in all His glory.

The thoughts of man, even the wisest of men, are so far from the thoughts and the ways of Elohim as to bear no positive correlation. In the words of a modern writer:

> "We are all of limited intelligence, and in the eyes of God the difference between the philosopher and the moron is no doubt immaterial."

Chapter 9

WISDOM

The beginning of wisdom is: Get wisdom
and in all your gettings, get understanding.
Proverbs

א] כִּי אֶת־כָּל־זֶה נָתַתִּי אֶל־לִבִּי וְלָבוּר אֶת־כָּל־זֶה אֲשֶׁר
הַצַּדִּיקִים וְהַחֲכָמִים וַעֲבָדֵיהֶם בְּיַד הָאֱלֹהִים גַּם־אַהֲבָה גַם־
שִׂנְאָה אֵין יוֹדֵעַ הָאָדָם הַכֹּל לִפְנֵיהֶם:

(א) ולבור. ולברר: **את־כל־זה.** ביררתי והבחנתי **אשר הצדיקים והחכמים ועבדיהם ביד האלהים,** הוא עוזרם והוא שופטם כדי להטיבם באחריתם: **ועבדיהם.** הם תלמידיהם משמשיהם, הולכי ארחותם: **גם־אהבה גם־שנאה אין יודעין** שאר הבריות ואין מכירין לתת לב במה יאהבו למקום ובמה הם שנואים: **הכל לפניהם.** לפני הצדיקים והחכמים:

1 / Special providence for the righteous

1] ALL THIS I MEDITATED UPON . . . All the attempts by man to explain the ways of Elohim. These have all been in vain (8:17).

THE RIGHTEOUS . . . IN THE HAND OF ELOHIM . . . Nevertheless it is clear to Koheleth from personal observation that the

CHAPTER NINE

1] All this I meditated upon, and it became clear that the righteous and the wise and all their works are in the hand of Elohim; though men cannot be certain either of love or of hate; all is before them.

righteous are in the hand of Elohim, i.e., that there is a special providence for the righteous, that it is not true that the same things happen to the righteous as to the wicked.

THOUGH MEN CANNOT BE CERTAIN . . . ALL IS BEFORE THEM. Though men, even righteous men, cannot be certain of Elohim's love or of Elohim's hate since all is before them — both good and evil — nevertheless from his experience Koheleth is convinced that the righteous receive special consideration during their earthly sojourn.

ב] הַכֹּל כַּאֲשֶׁר לַכֹּל מִקְרֶה אֶחָד לַצַּדִּיק וְלָרָשָׁע לַטּוֹב
וְלַטָּהוֹר וְלַטָּמֵא וְלַזֹּבֵחַ וְלַאֲשֶׁר אֵינֶנּוּ זֹבֵחַ כַּטּוֹב כַּחֹטֶא
הַנִּשְׁבָּע כַּאֲשֶׁר שְׁבוּעָה יָרֵא׃
ג] זֶה רָע בְּכֹל אֲשֶׁר־נַעֲשָׂה תַּחַת הַשֶּׁמֶשׁ כִּי־מִקְרֶה אֶחָד לַכֹּל
וְגַם לֵב בְּנֵי־הָאָדָם מָלֵא־רָע וְהוֹלֵלוֹת בִּלְבָבָם בְּחַיֵּיהֶם
וְאַחֲרָיו אֶל־הַמֵּתִים׃
ד] כִּי־מִי אֲשֶׁר יבחר [יְחֻבַּר] אֶל כָּל־הַחַיִּים יֵשׁ בִּטָּחוֹן כִּי־
לְכֶלֶב חַי הוּא טוֹב מִן־הָאַרְיֵה הַמֵּת׃

(ב) **הכל כאשר לכל.** **הכל** נותנים ללבם **כאשר** מגיע **לכל** אדם, שסוף דבר לתת לכל איש כדרכיו: מקרה **אחד.** ויודעים שסוף הכל — אשר צדיק ואשר רשע — למות, ומקרה אחד יש בעולם הזה לכולם; כל זה הם יודעים ואף על פי כן בוחרים להם דרך הטוב, לפי שיודעים שיש הפרש ביניהם לעולם הבא: **לצדיק** — כגון נח, **ולרשע** — פרעה נכה, זה נצלע וזה נצלע; **לטוב** — זה משה, **ולטהור** — זה אהרן, **ולטמא** — אלו מרגלים, אלו אמרו שבחה של ארץ ישראל ואלו אמרו גנותה, אלו לא נכנסו לארץ ואלו לא נכנסו לארץ; הרי מקרה אחד להם: **ולזבח** — זה יאשיהו, שנאמר (דברי הימים ב׳ לה: ז) (ויזבח) [וירם] יאשיהו וגומר, **ולאשר איננו זבח** — זה אחאב שביטל את ישראל מעלות לרגל, זה מת בחצים וזה מת בחצים; **כטוב** — זה דוד, **כחוטא** — זה נבוכדנצר, זה בנה בית המקדש וזה החריבו, זה מלך ארבעים שנה וזה מלך ארבעים שנה; **(כנשבע) [הנשבע]** — זה צדקיהו שנשבע לשקר, שנאמר (דברי הימים ב׳ לו: יג) וגם במלך נבוכדנאצר מרד אשר השביעו וגומר, **כאשר שבועה ירא** — זה שמשון, שנאמר (שופטים טו: יב) ויאמר (אליהם) [להם] שמשון השבעו לי פן־תפגעון בי אתם, למדנו שהיתה שבועה חמורה לו, זה מת בניקור עינים וזה מת בניקור עינים (ויקרא רבה פ״כ א; וע׳ תנחומא ואתחנן א); על כן (ג) **לב בני־האדם מלא־רע,** שאומרים אין דין פורענות [לרשעים], אין הכל אלא לפי המקרה — פעמים לצדיק ופעמים לרשע, **ואחריו אל־המתים.** וסופן יורדים לגיהנם: (ד) **כי־מי אשר (יבחר)** [קרי **יחבר**] **אל כל־החיים יש בטחון.** כי בעודו בחיים, אפילו הוא רשע ונתחבר לרשעים, כמו

2–6 / The ultimate for the non-believer — death

2] ALL THINGS COME ALIKE TO ALL . . . Having closed the previous verse with "all is before them," namely, that good and evil is the lot of all, both righteous and wicked, Koheleth

2] All things come alike to all; the same things happen to the righteous as to the wicked; to the good and pure as to the impure; to him who brings offerings as to him who does not; as with the good man so with the sinner; as with the man who takes his oath lightly so with the man who fears an oath.

3] This is an evil in all that is done under the sun — that the same fate should come to all; therefore, the hearts of men are filled with evil and madness during their lifetime — for afterwards they join the dead.

4] "Is he who is joined to all of life sure of the hereafter? Rather a living dog than a dead lion.

proceeds to relate how this fact affects the thinking of the non-believer, and verse 3 relates how these conclusions lead to evil practice. In verses 4, 5 and 6, Koheleth actually paraphrases the non-believer.

3] AFTERWARDS THEY JOIN THE DEAD. The joy of the non-believer is not an unmixed pleasure, for subconsciously, at least, he looks forward only to death. Nevertheless, death serves as an alibi for him to seek the maximum of pleasure during his lifetime. Since he believes there is no hereafter and everything terminates with death, he might as well pamper his passions even if it involves evil and madness.

4] IS HE ... SURE OF THE HEREAFTER? Koheleth paraphrases the non-believer who now asks sarcastically, "How sure is the believer that there is a hereafter?"

ה) כִּי הַחַיִּים יוֹדְעִים שֶׁיָּמֻתוּ וְהַמֵּתִים אֵינָם יוֹדְעִים מְאוּמָה
וְאֵין־עוֹד לָהֶם שָׂכָר כִּי נִשְׁכַּח זִכְרָם:
ו) גַּם אַהֲבָתָם גַּם־שִׂנְאָתָם גַּם־קִנְאָתָם כְּבָר אָבָדָה וְחֵלֶק אֵין־
לָהֶם עוֹד לְעוֹלָם בְּכֹל אֲשֶׁר־נַעֲשָׂה תַּחַת הַשָּׁמֶשׁ:

שנאמר אל כל־החיים — אפילו לרשעים — יש בטחון, שמא ישוב לפני מותו, **כי־לכלב חי הוא טוב מן־האריה המת,** ושניהם רשעים; טוב היה לו לנבוזראדן שהיה עבד רשע ונתגייר, שלא הקדימתו מיתה, מנבוכדנאצר רבו שנקרא אריה, שנאמר (ירמיה ד: ז) עלה אריה מסובכו, ומת ברשעו בגיהנם, ועבדו בגן עדן. ורבותינו דרשו (שבת ל ע״ב) לענין מחתכין את הנבילה לפני הכלבים בשבת (שם קנו ע״ב), ומת המוטל בחמה אסור לטלטלו אלא אם כן הניחו עליו תינוק או ככר (שם מג ע״ב): (ה) **כי החיים יודעים שימתו.** ואולי ישיבו אל לבם יום המיתה וישובו מדרכם, אבל משמתו אינם יודעים מאומה ואין עוד להם שכר פעולה שיעשו מן המיתה ואילך, אלא מי שטרח בערב שבת יאכל בשבת (עבודה זרה ג ע״א): (ו) **גם אהבתם** שאהבו פתי ולצון, **גם־שנאתם** ששנאו דעת, **גם־קנאתם** שהקניאו להקדוש ברוך הוא במעשה ידיהם: **וחלק אין־להם וגו׳ בכל אשר־נעשה וגו׳.** לא הועיל להם זכות בן ובת לאותן רשעים שעבדו עבודה זרה, ואין להם כפרה לאחר מיתה:

HE WHO IS JOINED TO ALL OF LIFE . . . The believer, who subscribes to the idea that life does not terminate with death; that there are two forms of life, one in this world and one in the hereafter.

RATHER A LIVING DOG . . . "One should give vent to his passions in this world, and not look forward to reward in another world," says the cynic. The non-believer emphasizes his denial

5] "The only thing the living are sure of is — death. The dead know nothing. There is no further reward for them, for their memory is forgotten.

6] "Their loves, their hates and their jealousies — all have perished. They have lost forever any part in whatever is done under the sun."

of the hereafter by comparing himself (the weaker morally) to the weaker dog and the believer (the stronger morally) to the strong lion. He implies, "What has the believer gained by showing his moral strength in restraining his passions? Now, after his demise, he is just a dead lion. I'd rather be a living dog than a dead lion."

5] THE ONLY THING ... SURE ... IS DEATH. The non-believer continues in his cynicism. He knows only what he sees. He sees death; he does not see the hereafter.

THERE IS NO FURTHER REWARD ... Therefore, why deny yourself the pleasure of passion? Why help the poor and the needy? Why abide by moral standards and morality? There is no further reward. Only the living have rewards and enjoyments.

6] ALL HAVE PERISHED ... In the eyes of the non-believer, everything terminates with death.

ז לֵךְ אֱכֹל בְּשִׂמְחָה לַחְמֶךָ וּשְׁתֵה בְלֶב־טוֹב יֵינֶךָ כִּי כְבָר
רָצָה הָאֱלֹהִים אֶת־מַעֲשֶׂיךָ:
ח בְּכָל־עֵת יִהְיוּ בְגָדֶיךָ לְבָנִים וְשֶׁמֶן עַל־רֹאשְׁךָ אַל־יֶחְסָר:
ט רְאֵה חַיִּים עִם־אִשָּׁה אֲשֶׁר־אָהַבְתָּ כָּל־יְמֵי חַיֵּי הֶבְלֶךָ אֲשֶׁר
נָתַן־לְךָ תַּחַת הַשֶּׁמֶשׁ כֹּל יְמֵי הֶבְלֶךָ כִּי הוּא חֶלְקְךָ בַּחַיִּים
וּבַעֲמָלְךָ אֲשֶׁר־אַתָּה עָמֵל תַּחַת הַשָּׁמֶשׁ:

(ז) **לך אכל בשמחה.** אבל אתה הצדיק, שכבר רצה הקדוש ברוך הוא מעשיך הטובים ותזכה לעולם הבא — לך אכול בשמחה: (ח) **בכל־עת יהיו בגדיך לבנים.** התקן עצמך בכל שעה במעשה טוב, שאם תמות היום תיכנס בשלום. ומשל שלמה החכם את הדבר לאדם שהזמינו המלך ליום סעודה ולא קבע לו זמן, אם חכם הוא או פיקח מיד מכבס כסותו ורוחץ וסך, וכן עת מחר, עד עת יקרא אל הסעודה יהיו כל שעה בגדיו לבנים, והוא רחוץ וסך; כך דרשוהו רבותינו במסכת שבת (קנג ע״א): (ט) **ראה חיים עם־אשה אשר־אהבת.** ראה והבן ללמוד אומנות להתפרנס ממנו עם תלמוד תורה אשר בידך: **כי הוא חלקך בחיים.** אם עשית כן, יהיה חלקך זה חיים בעולם הזה להתפרנס מן האומנות ובעולם הבא (ע׳ קידושין ל ע״ב), שיגיעת שניהם משכחת עון (אבות פ״ב מ״ב):

7–10 / The ultimate for the believer — life

7] Go . . . IN JOY . . . WITH A MERRY HEART . . . Koheleth now turns to the believer and urges him neither to pause nor to ponder because of frustration, anomalies, or the cynicism of the non-believer. Go — enjoy life, for that is what Elohim wants of man (see verse 3:22). Do not ponder, do not pause because you do not understand. It is useless to try to comprehend the inscrutable. Go — you know how to discount your afflictions; you know how to be content with what you have; you can really enjoy life. The joy of the non-believer is tainted by doom, by his conviction that everything terminates with death. The materialist is never completely happy because he is never satisfied with what he has. Only you, the believer, can be truly happy because you look forward to a cheerful future, a hereafter. You can reap the most out of life — life in two worlds.

7] Go, eat your bread in joy, and drink your wine with a merry heart. Elohim has already accepted your deeds.

8] Let your garments always be white, and let your head lack no oil.

9] Enjoy life with the wife whom you love all the days of the life of your vanity which Elohim has given you under the sun, all the days of your vanity, for that is your portion in life and in your toil wherein you toil under the sun.

ELOHIM HAS ALREADY ACCEPTED YOUR DEEDS. Elohim wants you to enjoy life. Therefore, if your attitude toward life has brought you satisfaction and your deeds have brought you a maximum of enjoyment, know that Elohim has given prior approval to your way of life.

8] LET YOUR GARMENTS ... BE WHITE ... A parenthetical verse. Though Elohim wishes you to enjoy life and to partake of His many blessings, He asks that you maintain your moral integrity and not stain your worth or dignity — let your garments be white.

LET YOUR HEAD LACK NO OIL. Oil was used to anoint kings; it symbolized nobility. In your dealings with men, show nobility of character. In your enjoyment of worldly goods, do not be voracious or voluptuous; do not become a slave to the material. Always remember that the oil of nobility rests on your head.

9] ENJOY LIFE WITH THE WIFE WHOM YOU LOVE. Koheleth sees in wife and family the greatest source of joy for man in his sojourn under the sun and in his struggle for existence

י כָּל אֲשֶׁר תִּמְצָא יָדְךָ לַעֲשׂוֹת בְּכֹחֲךָ עֲשֵׂה כִּי אֵין מַעֲשֶׂה
וְחֶשְׁבּוֹן וְדַעַת וְחָכְמָה בִּשְׁאוֹל אֲשֶׁר אַתָּה הֹלֵךְ שָׁמָּה:

(י) כל אשר תמצא ידך לעשות רצון קונך בעוד שאתה בכחך — **עשה, כי אין מעשה וגו' בשאול** לזכותך משתמות, ואם עשית כן, אין לך שום חשבון בשאול שתדאג ממנו; וכן המקרא מסורס — כי אין מעשה ודעת וחכמה בשאול לרשעים, ולא חשבון לצדיקים כשיתנו החוטאים דין וחשבון; וכך נדרש במדרש (ע' קה"ר). והבא לפותרו בלא סירוס, כמשמעו, פותר חשבון — לשון מחשבה, מה יוכל עוד לעשות להפטר מן הדין:

under the sun. Because of the frustrations and afflictions that every man is subject to, there is a need for the strength and security that only a wife and family can provide. Man has need of a companion, one to whom he can always turn — that is a wife. Man has need for someone with whom he can share his sorrows and troubles — that is a wife. Man needs someone who will love him in spite of his faults — that is a wife. The joys of the home, the family, are needed in order to face each day with renewed vigor.

ALL THE DAYS . . . OF YOUR VANITY . . . ALL THE DAYS . . . Emphasis is placed on all the days, because man needs companionship all his days. Each day has its blessings and its curses; good and evil is shared by everybody. There is need for the support of a companion in facing the trials of each day.

VANITY . . . In Koheleth's eyes anything less than the perfect is vanity. Therefore, man's days under the sun, mixed as they are with joy and sadness, are days of vanity.

10] Whatever you are able to do, do with all your might, for there is neither deed, nor planning, nor knowledge, nor wisdom in the grave toward which you are heading.

WHICH ELOHIM HAS GIVEN YOU . . . Each day of life, each moment that man breathes, is a gift of Elohim and must be counted among man's blessings.

THAT IS YOUR PORTION IN LIFE . . . a lifelong companion, a family of love and loved ones to bring pleasantness into a life of toil.

10] WHATEVER YOU ARE ABLE TO DO . . . Again, a parenthetical remark. If you have faith, you can enjoy this world and the hereafter. But remember, if you are going to perform good deeds, do them in this world. For the world of the hereafter is only a world of reward. The reward in the hereafter is in proportion to the quality of the good you have performed in this world. Therefore, if you are planning to improve yourself morally and spiritually, if you contemplate doing good deeds in behalf of your fellow man, then do these things here and now with all your might. There is joy in the knowledge that you have advanced spiritually; there is joy in the knowledge that you have helped your fellow-man; and there is also joy in the knowledge that you will be rewarded in the hereafter.

יא] שַׁבְתִּי וְרָאֹה תַחַת־הַשֶּׁמֶשׁ כִּי לֹא לַקַּלִּים הַמֵּרוֹץ וְלֹא
לַגִּבּוֹרִים הַמִּלְחָמָה וְגַם לֹא לַחֲכָמִים לֶחֶם וְגַם לֹא לַנְּבֹנִים
עֹשֶׁר וְגַם לֹא לַיֹּדְעִים חֵן כִּי־עֵת וָפֶגַע יִקְרֶה אֶת־כֻּלָּם:
יב] כִּי גַּם לֹא־יֵדַע הָאָדָם אֶת־עִתּוֹ כַּדָּגִים שֶׁנֶּאֱחָזִים בִּמְצוֹדָה
רָעָה וְכַצִּפֳּרִים הָאֲחֻזוֹת בַּפָּח כָּהֵם יוּקָשִׁים בְּנֵי הָאָדָם לְעֵת
רָעָה כְּשֶׁתִּפּוֹל עֲלֵיהֶם פִּתְאֹם:

(יא) **שבתי וראה.** כמו זכור, ווא״ונט בלעז (**vaant**, looking): **לא לקלים המרוץ.** לא עמדה לעשהאל קלותו משהגיע פקודתו: **ולא לגבורים המלחמה.** לא עמדה לאבנר גבורתו משהגיע יומו: **וגם לא לחכמים לחם.** כגון אני, שהיה לחמי ליום (מלכים א׳ ה:ב) שלשים כר סלת וגו׳ ועכשיו (קהלת ב:י) זה היה חלקי מכל עמלי — מקלי ומקידה: **וגם לא לנבנים עשר.** כגון איוב; בתחלה (איוב א:ג) ויהי מקנהו וגומר, כשבאה שעתו אמר (שם יט:כא) חנני אתם רעי: **וגם לא לידעים חן.** הרי משה, אין יודע ונבון ממנו בישראל, ולא מצא חן בתפלתו שיכנס לארץ (ע׳ תנחומא ואתחנן ב): **כי־עת ופגע.** כמשמעו. דבר אחר, כי עת יקרה אותם והפגיעה והתחינה יהיו רגילין בהם, שלא יבואו לדברים הללו: (יב) **כדגים שנאחזים במצודה רעה.** כדגים גדולים, שנאחזים במצודה גרועה וחלושה; ופירשו רבותינו (ע׳ קה״ר) — היא חכה, שאינה אלא כמין מחט, ודג גדול נלכד בה: **כהם יוקשים בני האדם.** במכשול קטן וחלש כמו המצודה הרעה והפח נכשלים בני אדם בעת פקודת רעתם, כשבא עתם ליפול הרעה עליהם פתאום במצודה רעה — מלאוויש״א בלעז (**mallvajjse**, evil): **כהם.** כמותם:

11–12 / The anomalies of success and longevity

11] Again, it became clear to me . . . Another case of apparent injustice that gives the non-believer an alibi for rebellion. There seems to be no logical justification for the success of some people or for their longevity. Many talented people suffer failure and many a virtuous man dies at an early age.

nor is bread won by the wise . . . Just as worldly goods are not always granted to the righteous, so is success not always achieved by the wise. There are rich persons who are simpletons and there are wise persons who are poor; there

11] Again, it became clear to me, under the sun, that the race is not won by the swift, nor the battle by the brave, nor is bread won by the wise, nor riches by the clever, nor favor by the learned. All seem subject to time and chance.

12] Man, also, does not know his time; as fish that are taken in an evil net, as birds that are caught in the snare, so are men snared in an evil time, when it falls upon them suddenly.

are diligent ones whose possessions are meager, and there are indolent ones who are wealthy.

ALL SEEM SUBJECT TO TIME AND CHANCE . . . To the human mind it appears that the distribution of success is haphazard; that it is a question of luck, of timing or of chance, rather than the result of merit.

12] MAN, ALSO, DOES NOT KNOW HIS TIME . . . In the matter of length of years, likewise, man is frequently subject to sudden death. Life is full of apparent inequities and uncertainties in this respect. In vain does man seek to find an explanation of why some die young and others live to a ripe old age.

These anomalies, added to those mentioned earlier by Koheleth, serve as alibis for the non-believer to continue in his pleasure-seeking pursuits without moral restraints. The believer sees in the anomalies a challenge through which Elohim tests the man of faith; the non-believer sees in them a world dictated by haphazard natural forces. The non-believer takes his clue from the evil in the universe to indulge irresponsibly in pleasure; the believer takes his clue from the good in the universe to go and live, and enjoy life responsibly.

יג] גַּם־זֹה רָאִיתִי חָכְמָה תַּחַת הַשָּׁמֶשׁ וּגְדוֹלָה הִיא אֵלָי׃

יד] עִיר קְטַנָּה וַאֲנָשִׁים בָּהּ מְעָט וּבָא־אֵלֶיהָ מֶלֶךְ גָּדוֹל וְסָבַב
אֹתָהּ וּבָנָה עָלֶיהָ מְצוֹדִים גְּדֹלִים׃

טו] וּמָצָא בָהּ אִישׁ מִסְכֵּן חָכָם וּמִלַּט־הוּא אֶת־הָעִיר בְּחָכְמָתוֹ
וְאָדָם לֹא זָכַר אֶת־הָאִישׁ הַמִּסְכֵּן הַהוּא׃

טז] וְאָמַרְתִּי אָנִי טוֹבָה חָכְמָה מִגְּבוּרָה וְחָכְמַת הַמִּסְכֵּן בְּזוּיָה
וּדְבָרָיו אֵינָם נִשְׁמָעִים׃

יז] דִּבְרֵי חֲכָמִים בְּנַחַת נִשְׁמָעִים מִזַּעֲקַת מוֹשֵׁל בַּכְּסִילִים׃

(טו) **ואדם לא זכר.** לא היה חושבו לכלום; (טז) **ואמרתי אני,** בראותי כן, **טובה חכמה מגבורה.** והרי חכמתו של זה בזויה לכולם, ועכשיו כולם נמלטו על ידו. ומדרש אגדה (מדרש תהלים מא: א; נדרים לב ע״ב) (יד) **עיר קטנה** — זה הגוף, **ואנשים בה מעט** — אלו איבריו של אדם, **מלך גדול** — זה יצר הרע, שכל איבריו מרגישים בו, (טו) **איש מסכן** — [זה] יצר טוב: (יז) **בנחת נשמעים.** מקובלים הם לבריות **מזעקת מושל בכסילים.** מלכי האומות. משה נפטר זה כמה שנים, ועדיין גזירותיו מקובלים על ישראל; וכמה מלכי האומות

13–18 / Wisdom saved city — poor man forgotten

13] I HAVE SEEN IN REGARD TO WISDOM . . . Koheleth is unwavering in his passion and praise for wisdom and now he returns once more to the subject.

AND IT IS SIGNIFICANT TO ME. There is an important lesson to be learnt from the story.

14] A SMALL CITY WITH FEW PEOPLE . . . To emphasize that there was no chance to save the city by brute strength.

15] BUT THERE WAS . . . A POOR WISE MAN . . . Koheleth accentuates the fact that the wise man was forgotten because of the deplorable human tendency to hold the poor in low regard.

13] This too I have seen in regard to wisdom, under the sun, and it is significant to me.

14] There was a small city, with few people in it, and there came a great king against it and beleagured it and built great bulwarks against it.

15] But there was found in it a poor wise man who saved the city by his wisdom. Yet no one remembered that poor man.

16] And so I say, wisdom is more powerful than strength, even though the wisdom of the poor man is despised and his words go unheeded.

17] The words of the wise, spoken in quiet, are more effective than the shouting of a ruler to fools.

16] WISDOM IS MORE POWERFUL THAN STRENGTH. An important lesson derived from the story is that wisdom is man's best guide — that wisdom is more powerful than strength — and yet, the wise man is forgotten.

THE WISDOM OF THE POOR MAN IS DESPISED . . . After having seen that the city was saved by wisdom, one would have thought that the people would turn to the wise man for advice in their daily living. This would have been logical. But logic does not dictate action for pleasure-seeking people. They utilize the wise man in a state of emergency; otherwise he is despised, especially when he is poor.

17] THE WORDS OF THE WISE . . . A ruler will be more effective if he utilizes wisdom than if he rules by force. When a ruler reasons in quiet, his people gain insight and understanding. Consequently, when they are called on to perform they do so willingly and understandingly. However, when a

יח) טוֹבָה חָכְמָה מִכְּלֵי קְרָב וְחוֹטֶא אֶחָד יְאַבֵּד טוֹבָה הַרְבֵּה:

גוזרים גזירות על ישראל, ואין דבריהם מתקיימין: **(יח) טובה חכמה מכלי קרב.** חכמתה של סרח, שנאמר (שמואל ב׳ כ:כב) ותבוא האשה אל [כל] העם בחכמתה, עמדה להם יותר מכלי קרב שהיה בידם להלחם עם יואב; **וחוטא אחד יאבד טובה הרבה.** אילולי שהרגה לשבע בן בכרי היו כולם אבודים על ידו (תנחומא ב׳ וירא אות יב, וע׳ קה״ר). דבר אחר, **וחוטא אחד יאבד טובה הרבה** — הרי שהיו ישראל מחצה צדיקים ומחצה רשעים ובא אחד וחטא ועשאן מרובין, נמצא שהכריע את כולם לחובה (קדושין מ ע״ב):

ruler shouts at his followers they obey only out of fear but like fools they lack understanding. They do not possess the motivation provided by insight.

18] Wisdom is better than weapons of war, but one error may destroy a multitude of good.

18] WISDOM IS BETTER THAN WEAPONS OF WAR . . . This has been well illustrated by the above story. But one must consider that his opponent may also possess wisdom.

ONE ERROR MAY DESTROY . . . Therefore one must be circumspect and examine carefully both sides of the argument, for all the good ideas may fail as the result of one misjudgment.

Chapter 10

OPPRESSION

You have greedily gained from your neighbor
by oppression,
and you have forgotten Me, the Lord God.
Ezekiel

א] זְבוּבֵי מָוֶת יַבְאִישׁ יַבִּיעַ שֶׁמֶן רוֹקֵחַ יָקָר מֵחָכְמָה מִכָּבוֹד סִכְלוּת מְעָט:

ב] לֵב חָכָם לִימִינוֹ וְלֵב כְּסִיל לִשְׂמֹאלוֹ:

ג] וְגַם־בַּדֶּרֶךְ כשהסכל [כְּשֶׁסָּכָל] הֹלֵךְ לִבּוֹ חָסֵר וְאָמַר לַכֹּל סָכָל הוּא:

(א) **זבובי מות יבאיש יביע וגו׳.** כגון בימי החורף, שאין בזבובין כח והם קרובים למות, גם אם בא לתוך שמן רוקח ומתערב בבשמים הוא מבאיש והוא מעלה קצף, שקורין אשקומ״א בלעז (**askume**, foaming, froth) ונראה בו כמין אבעבועות וזהו משמעו של יביע, הרי דבר קל שהפסיד דבר חשוב — כך יקר מחכמה (ומכבוד) [מכבוד] סכלות מעט, שהרי הכריע את כולם; הרי שהיה אדם זה שקול במחצה עבירות ומחצה זכיות, ובא ועבר עבירה אחת והכריעתו לכף חובה (קדושין מ ע״ב, וע׳ ירושלמי שם פ״ח ה״ט), נמצאת סכלות זה שהוא דבר מועט יקר וכבד ושוקל יותר מכל החכמה והכבוד שהיה בו, שהרי הכריע את כולם. יקר. לשון כובד (הוא כבד ושוקל יותר מן החכמה וכבוד שבו). ומדרש אגדה (ברכות סא ע״א) מושלים יצר הרע לזבובי מות. **יבאיש יביע** שם טוב, שהוא ערב משמן רוקח (ע׳ קה״ר פ״ז א): (ב) **לב חכם לימינו.** חכמתו מזומנת להטותו אל דרך המיומנת לטובתו, **ולב כסיל לשמאלו,** לעקשו מן הדרך המיומנת, שהיא תפארת ונוחה לו: (ג) **ואמר לכל סכל הוא.** בהליכתו ובדבורו הכל מכירין שהוא שוטה:

1–3 / The wise man is cautious

1] Dead flies . . . literally, "flies of death." In a weakened condition flies land in the most unpredictable places and frequently, quite innocently, cause damage by deterioration. Likewise, the respect and honor accorded the wise man, the glory of the savant, may be denigrated by a little folly. The wise man, therefore, has to be very careful to maintain his dignity; he has to guard against behavior that may be interpreted as foolish.

1] Just as dead flies make the perfumer's ointment fetid and putrid, so a little folly can outweigh wisdom and honor.

2] The wise man's mind dominates as though it were on the right side; the fool's mind submits as though it were on the left side.

3] Even if a fool should set out upon a course, he is without reason all along the way and proclaims to all that he is a fool.

This verse follows in the spirit of the final verse of Chapter 9, wherein Koheleth warns that "one misjudgment can negate a multitude of good."

2] THE WISE MAN'S MIND DOMINATES . . . Koheleth draws the parallel: Just as in the average person the right side dominates over the left, so in the wise man the sober mind dominates over irrational passion. However, the fool permits himself to be guided by the irrational.

3] EVEN IF A FOOL SHOULD SET OUT UPON A COURSE . . . Even if a fool should on occasion set up a worthwhile goal for himself, his approach is unrealistic. He is not prepared to face the obstacles and frustrations in his path. Being without mind, he continually blunders. Thus he proclaims to all that he is a fool.

ד] אִם־רוּחַ הַמּוֹשֵׁל תַּעֲלֶה עָלֶיךָ מְקוֹמְךָ אַל־תַּנַּח כִּי מַרְפֵּא
יַנִּיחַ חֲטָאִים גְּדוֹלִים׃
ה] יֵשׁ רָעָה רָאִיתִי תַּחַת הַשָּׁמֶשׁ כִּשְׁגָגָה שֶׁיֹּצָא מִלִּפְנֵי הַשַּׁלִּיט׃
ו] נִתַּן הַסֶּכֶל בַּמְּרוֹמִים רַבִּים וַעֲשִׁירִים בַּשֵּׁפֶל יֵשֵׁבוּ׃
ז] רָאִיתִי עֲבָדִים עַל־סוּסִים וְשָׂרִים הֹלְכִים כַּעֲבָדִים עַל־
הָאָרֶץ׃

(ד) **אם־רוח המושל,** מושל העולם, תעלה עליך לדקדק אחריך במדת הדין — **מקומך אל־תנח.** מדתך הטובה אל תנח לומר לו מה יועיל צדקתי לי; **כי מרפא.** דקדוקי הדין ביסורין (הבאין) [הבא] עליך מרפא הוא לעונותיך, ויניח לך חטאים הגדולים: (ה) **כשגגה שיצא מלפני השליט.** דומה הוא לשליט שהוציא דבר שגגה מפיו, שוגג ואי אפשר לחזור — כך אומר הקדוש ברוך הוא ואין להשיב: (ו) **נתן הסכל במרומים רבים.** זו היא הרעה שהיא כשגגה שיוצא מלפני השליט, שניתן השטות והרשע במרומי גובה, שהגביה הקדוש ברוך הוא את הכסילים ואת הרשעים, שאני רואה ברוח הקדש שהם עתידים לפשוט יד בהיכלו ולשום אותותם אותות: **ועשירים בשפל ישבו.** ישראל שכל הגדולה והכבוד שיש להם עכשיו בימי, עתידים לישב בשפל, שנאמר (איכה ב: י) ישבו לארץ ידמו: (ז) **ראיתי עבדים על־סוסים.** כשדים הם (ע׳ תנחומא ב׳ וישב אות טו), שנאמר בהם (ישעיה כג: יג) זה העם לא היה — יתעלו להיות על סוסים, מוליכים את שבויי ישראל אסורים בקולרין **הולכים כעבדים על־הארץ,**

4–11 / Oppression brings its own punishment

4] If the urge to dominate . . . If you are attracted to a higher position because it will give you greater power to dominate over people — beware. There is no greater evil than to mistreat your fellow man. It is quite natural for man to desire to better his position for material gain or for prestigious and spiritual motives. But when the basis for changing one's position is the evil inclination to dominate over men, then one opens the door for the commission of many grave offenses.

Oppression of subordinates, lack of consideration for our fellow-man, using people as pawns, are offenses that can only boomerang upon the perpetrator.

4] If the urge to dominate should seize you, do not give up your position; for softness may open the door to grave offenses.

5] There is evil under the sun that is looked upon as though it were only an error emanating from the ruler.

6] Folly is enthroned upon great heights, but the rich sit in low places.

7] I have seen slaves on horses, while lords walk on foot like slaves.

Therefore, if you are seized by the urge to dominate, bethink yourself. Perhaps you would do better to hold on to your present, less prominent position. To succumb to the urge for domination is to open the door to the gravest of evils — human oppression.

5] THERE IS EVIL . . . Koheleth illustrates by citing the example of a king who was ruthless with his subordinates.
AN ERROR EMANATING FROM THE RULER . . . After the injustice is uncovered, the ruler pretends that it was only an error.

6] FOLLY IS ENTHRONED . . . The ruler, who seeks to dominate over people, recognizes people only as pawns. If it serves his purposes, he seats even fools in high places and demotes the rich though they may be the more competent for the higher positions.

7] SLAVES ON HORSES . . . Though the slaves may never have had the training or education needed for the higher positions, they are appointed by the ruthless ruler to dominate over the well-trained and better-educated lords.

ח] חֹפֵר גּוּמָּץ בּוֹ יִפּוֹל וּפֹרֵץ גָּדֵר יִשְּׁכֶנּוּ נָחָשׁ:
ט] מַסִּיעַ אֲבָנִים יֵעָצֵב בָּהֶם בּוֹקֵעַ עֵצִים יִסָּכֶן בָּם:
י] אִם־קֵהָה הַבַּרְזֶל וְהוּא לֹא־פָנִים קִלְקַל וַחֲיָלִים יְגַבֵּר
וְיִתְרוֹן הַכְשֵׁיר חָכְמָה:

לפני קרונין של כשדים: (ח) **חפר גומץ**, שוחה — **בו יפול**. פעמים שהוא נופל בו, כלומר, יש לך חורשׁ רעה וסופו לשוב עליו, בסוף שכלה זרעו של נבוכדנצר על ידי כלי בית המקדש, שנאמר (דניאל ה:כג) ועל מרא־שמיא התרוממת [וגומר]: **ופרץ גדר**, סייג של חכמים לעבור על דבריהם — **ישכנו נחש**. מיתה בידי שמים (שבת קי ע״א; ע״ז כז ע״ב). ולפי שדיבר בלשון פריצת גדר, הזכיר בתשלומין לשון נשיכת נחש, שהוא דר בחורי נקבי כתלי בתים פרוצים: (ט) **מסיע אבנים יעצב בהם**. מסיע אבנים ממחצבתם בהרים מתיגע בהם: **יעצב**. לשון יגיעה, כמו (בראשית ג:יז) בעצבון תאכלנה, כלומר כל אדם לפי מלאכתו עצבונו, אף עושה רעה — לפי זריעתו יקצור: **יסכן בם**. יתחמם בם, כמו (מלכים א׳ א:ב) ותהי־לו סכנת; אף העוסק בתורה ומצוות סופו ליהנות מהם (ע׳ סנהדרין ק ע״ב): (י) **אם־קהה הברזל**. חרבות צורים, שקיהו פיהם וחדודם, **והוא לא־פנים** קלקל. ואינם לטושים ומרוטים למען היות להם ברק (ע׳ יחזקאל כא:יד, טו) — אף על פי כן **וחילים יגבר**. מגביר הוא במלחמה את גבורי החיילים לנצח: **ויתרון הכשיר חכמה**. ומעלת כשרון יש עוד לחכמה יותר מן הברזל, אם תלמיד חכם משחירין פניו ברעב, ואתה רואהו מסכן בין העשירים, הרבה חיילים מתגברים על ידו (ע׳ תענית ח ע״א). ואל תתמה על וי״ו וחיילים, כי הרבה ווי״ן נופלים כן בלשון עברית, כמו (תהלים

8] He who digs a pit . . . When the autocratic ruler wants to dismiss a high-ranking officer, he "digs a pit" for him. He assigns to him an impossible task or he so manipulates the situation that the subordinate must fail.

Koheleth assures us that such a ruler will ultimately himself fall into the kind of pit he digs for his fellow-man. Koheleth inherited this sense of retribution in kind from his father, David (Psalms 7:16): "He dug a pit and hallowed it and fell into the ditch which he made."

WHO BREAKS THROUGH A FENCE WILL BE BITTEN BY A SNAKE. Snakes often hibernate among the stones in a fence and he

8] He who digs a pit will himself fall into it; he who breaks through a fence will be bitten by a snake.

9] He who removes stones will suffer because of them, and he who cuts logs endangers himself therewith.

10] If the axe is blunt and it is not sharpened beforehand, greater strength is needed to wield it, but it would have been wiser to prepare it beforehand.

who disturbs them is liable to be bitten. Likewise, he who breaks the moral code established between man and man is liable to punishment. The ruler who does not respect men and their cherished values will only reap the fruit of uprisings and vengeance.

9] HE WHO REMOVES STONES ... The ruler who removes men from their positions, who engenders uncertainty and despair among men, must needs suffer for his tyranny.

HE WHO CUTS LOGS ... He who cuts people down, who oppresses them or belittles them, only endangers his own position. Man must honor his fellow-man; to deprive men of their dignity breeds only resentment and revolution.

10] IF THE AXE IS BLUNT ... To place slaves, untrained persons, in responsible positions is as unsound as to try to fell trees with a blunt axe. Just as greater strength is needed in order to work with a blunt axe, so, much time, money and valuable energy is wasted by placing untrained and inept individuals in positions requiring skill and mastery, and then having to assist them.

יא] אִם־יִשֹּׁךְ הַנָּחָשׁ בְּלוֹא־לָחַשׁ וְאֵין יִתְרוֹן לְבַעַל הַלָּשׁוֹן:

נ: יח) אם־ראית גנב ותרץ עמו, (שמות טו: ב) עזי וזמרת יה ויהי־לי לישועה, והרבה מפורשים כזה: (יא) **אם־ישך הנחש את איש בלוא־לחש.** מחמת שלא לחשו החבר שלא ישוך: **ואין יתרון לחבר הרשע,** שהיה רגיל ללחשו בלא לחש, כך אם בני עירך נכשלים באיסורין מחמת שאין חכם דורש להם ומלמדם את חוקי התורה, אין יתרון לו בשתיקתו ולא ישתכר (ע׳ תענית שם).

IT WOULD HAVE BEEN WISER TO PREPARE IT . . . It would have been wiser for the dominating ruler to appoint trained

11] For if the snake is permitted to bite before it is charmed, there is no point in having a charmer.

individuals or to train individuals before placing any of them in a responsible position.

11] FOR IF THE SNAKE ... If people are permitted to function before having adequate preparation, there is no point in having trainers.

יב) דִּבְרֵי פִי־חָכָם חֵן וְשִׂפְתוֹת כְּסִיל תְּבַלְּעֶנּוּ׃
יג) תְּחִלַּת דִּבְרֵי־פִיהוּ סִכְלוּת וְאַחֲרִית פִּיהוּ הוֹלֵלוּת רָעָה׃
יד) וְהַסָּכָל יַרְבֶּה דְבָרִים לֹא־יֵדַע הָאָדָם מַה־שֶּׁיִּהְיֶה וַאֲשֶׁר
יִהְיֶה מֵאַחֲרָיו מִי יַגִּיד לוֹ׃
טו) עֲמַל הַכְּסִילִים תְּיַגְּעֶנּוּ אֲשֶׁר לֹא־יָדַע לָלֶכֶת אֶל־עִיר׃

(יב) **דברי פי־חכם חן** על שומעיהם ונשמעים לו, וטוב לו שנוטל גדולה עליהם: **ושפתות כסיל תבלענו.** זה המסית את חבירו מדרך טובה, כגון בלעם שפרץ גדרן של אומות, שגדרו עצמן מן העריות מדור המבול ואילך והוא יעץ להם להיות מפקירין נשותיהם לזנות (סנהדרין קו ע״א): (יג) **תחלת דברי־פיהו סכלות.** כשאמר לו הקדוש ברוך הוא (במדבר כב: ט) מי האנשים האלה עמך, היה לו להשיב — ה׳ אתה יודע, והוא אמר (שם שם י) בלק בן־צפור מלך מואב שלח אלי, כלומר, אם בעיניך אני נבזה, חשוב אני בעיני מלכי הארץ (ע׳ במדבר רבה בלק פ״כ ט); **ואחרית פיהו הוללות.** שיעמום וערבוב, (שם כד: יד) לכה איעצך — (משלי כד: יט) זמת אולת; (יד) **והסכל ירבה דברים.** שהיה מתפאר בעצמו, שהיה יודע דעת עליון (במדבר כד: טז); **כי לא־ידע האדם מה־שיהיה** לו לאחר זמן, שהרי הלך ליטול שכרו במדין ולא ידע שיפול בחרב (סנהדרין שם). ולפי פשוטו, **הסכל ירבה דברים,** גוזר ואומר מחר אעשה כן לפלוני, ואינו יודע מה יהיה מחר; **ואשר יהיה מאחריו מי יגיד לו,** כלומר, לא סוף דבר שאינו יודע מה יהיה לאחר זמן, אלא אף ההווה עכשיו **מאחריו,** שלא כנגד עיניו אלא מאחורי ערפו מרחוק, צריך הוא שיהא **מי יגיד לו:** (טו) **עמל הכסילים תיגענו.** כסילותם גורם להם עמל המייגען, אשר לא למדו דרכי מבואות העיר, ומתייגע ליכנס דרך פתחים ובצעי המים ויגע בטביעת רגליו בבוץ, כלומר, עצלות של עוזבי התורה גורם להם יגיעת עמל בגיהנם **אשר לא־ידע ללכת אל** נתיב אמת לפרוש מן העבירה, לפי שלא למד תורה, שנאמר (תהלים קיט: קה) נר־לרגלי (דבריך) [דברך]:

12–15 / Fools enter where angels fear to tread

12] THE WORDS OF THE WISE MAN . . . Back again to Koheleth's most cherished value — wisdom. The wise man calculates each word, and what he does say brings him favor in people's eyes; whereas the remarks of the fool only serve to destroy his regard in the eyes of men.

12] The words of the wise man win favor, whereas the lips of the fool consume him.

13] The beginning of the words of his mouth is foolishness, and the end of his talk is grievous madness.

14] The fool multiplies words, when in truth man does not know what will be, and who can tell him what will take place after him.

15] The efforts of the fool exhaust him, because he doesn't even know the way to a city.

13] THE BEGINNING OF THE WORDS . . . At first, the fool makes exorbitant claims; his predictions are unfounded and his goals unrealistic.

THE END OF HIS TALK . . . When his lack of logic is made known to him, he resorts to rationalizations which are even more confusing and tend to border on madness.

14] THE FOOL MULTIPLIES WORDS . . . While the words of the fool are inane, they have the peculiar characteristic of a chain reaction, calling forth more foolish remarks in their wake. Worst of all, he attempts to predict without any adequate basis. Not even the wise can know the future. The fool tackles the future and the esoteric when he cannot even grapple with the present and the simple.

15] THE EFFORTS OF THE FOOL EXHAUST HIM . . . The fool sets goals for himself that he cannot attain. He knows what he is aiming for, but he does not know how to get there. Naturally, under such circumstances, he exhausts himself wandering in blind alleyways and ending up nowhere. He knows of the city, but does not know how to get there.

טז אִי־לָךְ אֶרֶץ שֶׁמַּלְכֵּךְ נָעַר וְשָׂרַיִךְ בַּבֹּקֶר יֹאכֵלוּ׃
יז אַשְׁרֵיךְ אֶרֶץ שֶׁמַּלְכֵּךְ בֶּן־חוֹרִים וְשָׂרַיִךְ בָּעֵת יֹאכֵלוּ
בִּגְבוּרָה וְלֹא בַשְּׁתִי׃
יח בַּעֲצַלְתַּיִם יִמַּךְ הַמְּקָרֶה וּבְשִׁפְלוּת יָדַיִם יִדְלֹף הַבָּיִת׃
יט לִשְׂחוֹק עֹשִׂים לֶחֶם וְיַיִן יְשַׂמַּח חַיִּים וְהַכֶּסֶף יַעֲנֶה אֶת־הַכֹּל׃

(טז) **אי־לך ארץ שמלכך.** בזמן שמלכך ודייניך מתנהגים בנערות: (יז) **בגבורה ולא בשתי.** שעוסקין בגבורת החכמה והבינה, ולא בשתיית יין (שבת י ע״א): (יח) **בעצלתיים** (**ימך המקרה**), כשאדם מתעצל ואינו מתקן פרצה קטנה שבתקרת הבית, **ימך המקרה.** ישפל הבנין המקרה את הבית והמסכך עליו: **ידלף.** יטפטף דלף גשמים, כלומר, כשישראל מתעצלים בתורה הם נמקים ובית גאון עוזם חרב ומך (תענית ז ע״ב): (יט) **לשחוק עשים לחם.** לחדוות מזמוטי חתנים ומלכים עושים סעודה; וסתם סעודה גדולה קרויה לחם, כמו דאת אמר (דניאל ה: א) בלשאצר מלכא עבד לחם רב; ויין משקין בסעודה, אשר **ישמח החיים: והכסף יענה את הכל.** אם אין כסף אין סעודה, לפיכך לא יתעצל אדם מן המלאכה, כדי שיהא לו מה להוציא:

16–19 / Decay follows in the wake of the immature leader

16] Woe . . . if your king is a boy . . . Good leadership requires maturity of mind. If the leader is merely a "boy," decay will set in.

and your lords feast in the morning. The immature leader is not inclined to exert himself in matters of government, so he surrounds himself with ministers to carry out his functions. Lacking the proper supervision, the ministers are easy prey to gluttony. They prefer to feast in the morning rather than to tackle the real problems which beset the land.

16] Woe to you, O land, if your king is a boy and your lords feast in the morning.
17] Happy are you, O land, if your king is a noble man and your lords feast at the proper time, in strength and not in drunkenness.
18] Where there is slothfulness the ceiling will sink in, and where hands are slack the house will leak.
19] They think that revelry can substitute for bread; that wine will gladden life, and that money can solve all problems.

17] HAPPY ... IF YOUR KING IS ... NOBLE ... Conversely, if the leader sets the proper example of diligence and devotion to the problems of the land, the ministers will follow.

18] WHERE THERE IS SLOTHFULNESS ... Slothfulness at the top is contagious and the entire leadership is likely to be unconcerned with the problems of the people. Thus the whole national structure will decay.

19] REVELRY CAN SUBSTITUTE FOR BREAD ... A picture of corrupt selfish politicians under immature leadership. Every day becomes a day of revelry. Idleness brings on moral decay and the problems of the country are drowned in drunkenness. Money is used to buy off those individuals who would criticize their inept rule.

כ) גַּם בְּמַדָּעֲךָ מֶלֶךְ אַל־תְּקַלֵּל וּבְחַדְרֵי מִשְׁכָּבְךָ אַל־תְּקַלֵּל
עָשִׁיר כִּי עוֹף הַשָּׁמַיִם יוֹלִיךְ אֶת־הַקּוֹל וּבַעַל הכנפים
[כְּנָפַיִם] יַגִּיד דָּבָר:

(כ) **גם במדעך** (מלך), במחשבותיך בלא דיבור; גם — אפילו; **מלך אל־תקלל.** אל תרגיז למלכו של עולם (ויקרא רבה פל״ב ב). דבר אחר, כמשמעו — מלך בשר ודם: **עוף השמים.** נשמה הנתונה בך, שסופה לעוף על השמים; **ובעל כנפים.** מלאך המלווה אותך, כענין שנאמר (תהלים צא: יא) כי מלאכיו יצוה לך (תענית יא ע״א). ולפי משמעו — העוברים והשבים, יש לך לדאג מכל בריה, שמא יש שומעין ויגידו לאחרים:

20 / Better silence than criticism in secret

20] Even in your thoughts . . . An exaggeration, to stress the importance of being very cautious about secretly criticiz-

20] Do not curse the king, even in your thoughts, nor curse the rich man even in your bed-chamber; for a bird of the skies may carry your voice and a winged creature may reveal the matter.

ing those in power. One must be careful about voicing such criticism even in the exclusive presence of a close friend, for somehow or other it is bound to get back to the ruler. The best way to keep a matter secret is not to repeat it even to yourself.

Chapter 11

LIFE IS BEAUTIFUL

God, however, is not content
that you should be only calm and secure.
He has destined you for joy,
for pure, human, unalloyed joy.
Not for nothing does He cause
the flowers to bloom and the fruits to ripen.
He has "created the earth not to be a waste,"
a vale of tears and sighing, but to be
a beautiful and gladsome dwelling-place
for joyful and happy beings.

S. R. Hirsch

א] שַׁלַּח לַחְמְךָ עַל־פְּנֵי הַמָּיִם כִּי־בְרֹב הַיָּמִים תִּמְצָאֶנּוּ׃

(א) **שלח לחמך על־פני המים.** עשה טובה וחסד לאדם שיאמר לך לבך עליו אל תראנו עוד, כאדם שמשליך מזונותיו על פני המים, **כי־ברב הימים תמצאנו.** עוד ימים באים ותקבל תשלומיך. ראה מה נאמר ביתרו (שמות ב:כ) קראן לו ויאכל לחם, וסבור שהוא מצרי ולא יראנו עוד — מה היה סופו? נעשה (חתנו) [חותנו], ומלך על ישראל והכניסו תחת כנפי השכינה, וזכו בניו ובני בניו לישב בלשכת הגזית (סנהדרין קד ע״א; וע׳ שמות רבה פכ״ז ז):

1 / Good deeds are ultimately rewarded

1] Cast your bread upon the waters . . . In the performance of good deeds one should not aim at receiving a reward. One who performs a good deed should derive pleasure from the knowledge that he has risen above selfish concerns to a moment of altruism. Though the benefactor

1] Cast your bread upon the waters, for you shall find it after many days.

may never see the recipient again, he has meanwhile elevated himself spiritually. Nor should the fact that the recipient has not expressed his gratitude prevent the benefactor from helping others. Cast your bread upon the waters whenever you can be of help to your fellow-man, without harm to yourself.

FOR YOU SHALL FIND IT AFTER MANY DAYS . . . Though the object of the benefactor was not the reward, Koheleth assures him that in due time he will find compensation for his deeds. There will always be reward for kindness and graciousness; the reward may be either material or spiritual, or both.

ב) תֶּן־חֵלֶק לְשִׁבְעָה וְגַם לִשְׁמוֹנָה כִּי לֹא תֵדַע מַה־יִּהְיֶה רָעָה
עַל־הָאָרֶץ׃
ג) אִם־יִמָּלְאוּ הֶעָבִים גֶּשֶׁם עַל־הָאָרֶץ יָרִיקוּ וְאִם־יִפּוֹל עֵץ
בַּדָּרוֹם וְאִם בַּצָּפוֹן מְקוֹם שֶׁיִּפּוֹל הָעֵץ שָׁם יְהוּא׃
ד) שֹׁמֵר רוּחַ לֹא יִזְרָע וְרֹאֶה בֶעָבִים לֹא יִקְצוֹר׃

(ב) **תן־חלק לשבעה וגם לשמונה.** חלקת מלחמך ומשלך לשבעה צריכי חסד, חלק עוד לשמונה שיבואו אחריהם ואל תאמר די, **כי לא תדע מה־יהיה רעה.** שמא עוד ימים באים ותצטרך לכולם, אז תנצל על ידי הצדקה מן הרעה, ואם לא עכשיו אימתי! ורבותינו אמרו (עירובין מ ע״ב) **תן חלק לשבעה** — אלו שבעה ימי בראשית, תן אחד מהן חלק ליוצרך לנוח בשבת, **וגם לשמונה** — אלו ימי המילה. דבר אחר, תן חלק **לשבעה** קרבנות צבור של שבעת ימי הפסח, **וגם לשמונה** — של שמונת ימי החג, **כי לא תדע מה־יהיה רעה.** אם יחרב הבית ולא תקריבו עוד, ויועילו הראשונים; דבר אחר, **כי לא תדע מה־יהיה.** לא ידעת מה נגזר על הגשמים בחג, ויועילו הקרבנות ויבטלו גזירות רעות: (ג) **אם־ימלאו העבים גשם.** אם ראית עבים מלאים גשם, ידעת שסופם יריקו גשמיהם על הארץ, במקום שהטובה צומחת וניכרת, שם סופה לנוח; אף כן, דע **שאם־יפול עץ** וגומר. אם ישכון אדם חכם וצדיק בעיר או במדינה, מקום שישכון שם יהיו נראין מעשיו אחרי מותו וחכמותיו ומדות תרומיותיו ותשלם טובה ליושבי המקום על מנהג הטוב שהדריכם בדרך ישרה (ע׳ קה״ר): **יפול.** ישכון כמו (בראשית כה: יח) על פני כל אחיו נפל: **עץ.** תלמיד חכם, שמגין בזכותו כעץ המסיך על הארץ: (ד) **שמר רוח** — ממתין ומצפה עד **בא הרוח, לא יזרע.** פעמים ממתין ואינו בא: **וראה בעבים** — נותן עיניו בעבים, וכשרואה אותם קודרים, ירא לקצור מפני הגשמים, ולעולם **לא יקצור** לפי

2-6 / Your fortune is in Elohim's hands — but you must do your share

2] Divide your wealth . . . Do not put all your eggs in one basket. Your investments should be reasonable and sound, but spread out in many varied ventures. You can never know what calamities may be visited upon earth; which ventures will prosper and which will go to ruin.

2] Divide your wealth into seven, even eight parts, for you know not what calamity may come upon the earth.

3] When the clouds are filled with rain, they empty upon the earth; if a tree should fall in the south or in the north, where it falls there shall it be.

4] He who waits for the wind will never sow; he who looks to the clouds will never reap.

3] WHEN THE CLOUDS ARE FILLED WITH RAIN . . . Just as the results of the rains are unpredictable — in some places they bring blessing and in others destruction — so economic cycles and world events may reward some ventures but inflict heavy losses upon others.

IF A TREE SHOULD FALL . . . If an investment should fail in one area or another, accept your losses, but go on trying in other areas.

4] HE WHO WAITS FOR THE WIND . . . If the farmer always studies the winds and looks to the clouds to be certain before he sows, he will never sow and he will consequently not reap. There must be an element of risk. Likewise he who wants to be sure that he will make a profit before he invests will never invest. Certainty is assured to nobody in this world.

Man, of course, must not squander his funds in unsound investments or invest blindly in unknown ventures. He must be cautious and he must examine the facts as thoroughly as possible. Thereafter, he must leave his fortune in the hands of Elohim. There is no certainty.

(ה) כַּאֲשֶׁר אֵינְךָ יוֹדֵעַ מַה־דֶּרֶךְ הָרוּחַ כַּעֲצָמִים בְּבֶטֶן הַמְּלֵאָה
כָּכָה לֹא תֵדַע אֶת־מַעֲשֵׂה הָאֱלֹהִים אֲשֶׁר יַעֲשֶׂה אֶת־הַכֹּל:
(ו) בַּבֹּקֶר זְרַע אֶת־זַרְעֶךָ וְלָעֶרֶב אַל־תַּנַּח יָדֶךָ כִּי אֵינְךָ יוֹדֵעַ
אֵי זֶה יִכְשַׁר הֲזֶה אוֹ־זֶה וְאִם־שְׁנֵיהֶם כְּאֶחָד טוֹבִים:

שירא תמיד: (ה) **כאשר אינך יודע.** הרי זה מקרא מסורס, נדרש מסופו לראשו. **כאשר אינך יודע** עצמים בבטן המלאה — דברים הנסגרים והנעצמים בבטן שהיא מלאה — ואף על פי שבולטת לחוץ [אינך יודע מה בבטנה, כך] **אינך יודע דרך הרוח,** כלומר, ידיעות שתי אלו שוות, לא זו גלויה לך ולא זו גלויה לך, פעמים אתה סבור להכיר בעבים שיבא הרוח ואינו בא כאן, כי עובר והולך לו אל ארץ אחרת; והרי לשון זה כמו (בראשית יג: י) כגן־ה׳ כארץ מצרים, (ישעיה כד: ב) כשפחה כגברתה כקונה כמוכר; ופעמים שהוא משוה מוקדם למאוחר ופעמים שהוא משוה מאוחר למוקדם, אף כאן למד ידיעת הרוח מידיעת הבטן, כלומר, אין לך לשמור את הרוח לראות בעבים. **כעצמים.** אנקלו״ש בלעז (enclos, enclosed) כמו (ישעיה לז: טו) יצם עיניו: **ככה לא תדע וגומר.** אף גזירותיו של מקום לעניין עניות ועשירות כך עלומות הם ממך, ולא תמנע מן החסד לדאג שמא אחסר מנכסי ואעני, לא אעסוק בתורה ואתבטל ממלאכתי ואעני, לא אשא אשה ויהיו לי בנים ואצטרך להוציא עליהם: (ו) **בבקר זרע את־זרעך** וגומר. אם למדת תורה בילדותך, למד תורה בזקנותך; אם היו לך תלמידים בילדותך, יהיו לך תלמידים בזקנותך; נשאת אשה בת בנים בילדותך, שא אשה בת בנים בזקנותך; עשית צדקה בילדותך, עשה צדקה בזקנותך; **כי אינך יודע אי זה יכשר.** אם תלמידים ובנים שבילדותך יתקיימו לך, או שמא לא יתקיימו אלא שבזקנותך. מצינו ברבי עקיבא, שהיו לו עשרים וארבעה אלף תלמידים מגבת ועד אנטיפרס וכולן מתו מפסח ועד עצרת, ובא אצל רבותינו שבדרום ושנאה להם (יבמות סב ע״ב). ולענין הבנים מצינו באבצן, (שופטים יב: ט) [ויהי־לו שלשים בנים] ושלשים בנות שלח החוצה ושלשים בנות הביא לבניו [מן־החוץ], וכולן מתו בחייו (בבא בתרא צא ע״א); ובזקנותו הוליד את עובד ונתקיים לו:

5] Just as you do not know the way of the wind, just as you do not know the formation of the embryonic structure in the mother's womb, so do you not know the working of Elohim Who makes everything.

6] Therefore, in the morning sow your seed and do not remain idle in the evening; for you cannot know whether the one will prosper or the other, or whether both will have equal success.

5] JUST AS YOU DO NOT KNOW ... THE WIND ... What causes winds or what will be the course of the wind. Just as you do not know winds or the formation of embryos, so you should not attempt to fathom the ways of Elohim and how He apportions wealth to each member of the human race.

The wind, the embryo, the economic cycle and world governments are all in the hands of Elohim, who makes everything. Your dependence must not be on your investments or on your fellowman, but upon Elohim alone.

6] THEREFORE, IN THE MORNING ... Morning refers to the early years and evening to the later years. Do not depend in your later years on investments made in your early years. Times change and you never know which will prosper better. And there is always the chance that you may succeed in both. Therefore, do not remain idle in the evening, in your later years.

ז וּמָתוֹק הָאוֹר וְטוֹב לָעֵינַיִם לִרְאוֹת אֶת־הַשָּׁמֶשׁ:
ח כִּי אִם־שָׁנִים הַרְבֵּה יִחְיֶה הָאָדָם בְּכֻלָּם יִשְׂמָח וְיִזְכֹּר אֶת־
יְמֵי הַחֹשֶׁךְ כִּי־הַרְבֵּה יִהְיוּ כָּל־שֶׁבָּא הָבֶל:
ט שְׂמַח בָּחוּר בְּיַלְדוּתֶךָ וִיטִיבְךָ לִבְּךָ בִּימֵי בְחוּרוֹתֶךָ וְהַלֵּךְ

(ז) **ומתוק האור.** מתוק הוא אורה של תורה, **וטוב לעינים לראות את־השמש.** ואשריהם התלמידים שעיניהם רואים הלכה מלובנת ומחוורת על בוריה — כך נדרש באגדת תהלים (מט: א־ב): (ח) **בכלם ישמח.** יהי שמח בחלקו, ובלבד שיזכר **את־ימי החשך** וייטיב מעשיו שינצל מהם, והם ימי מיתת עולם, הם ימי הרשעים, **כי־הרבה** יהיו באותן הימים יותר מימי החיים; **כל־שבא** עליו יהיה הבל וחשך. יש הבל שהוא לשון פורענות וצרות, כמו (לעיל ו: ד) כי־בהבל בא ובחשך ילך: (ט) **שמח בחור בילדותך.** כאדם שאומר לעבדו ולבנו חטא חטא, כי פעם אחת תלקה על הכל; אף כאן החכם אמר **שמח בחור בילדותך** ...

7–10 / Life is beautiful

From here to the end of the book, Koheleth stresses that man could and should be happy, in spite of the fact that life "under the sun" has its share of evil for everybody. The evil of the world is recognizable in two forms: (1) the ever-present frustrations and inequities; and (2) the oncoming of old age and debility.

Faith implies that man will see the good in the universe and count his blessings. He will strive to be content and happy in spite of adversities.

Before the darkness of old age approaches is the time to make the most out of life. Man should enjoy life to the utmost and yet remember that he is accountable for his deeds. In these final verses, Koheleth emphasizes the light of life, the darkness of old age, and man's responsibility for his deeds. The essence of his message is: Enjoy life, but at the same time remember Elohim and obey His commandments.

7] And the light is sweet; and it is a pleasant thing for the eyes to see the sun.

8] For if a man live many years, let him rejoice in them all and remember that the days of darkness will be many. All that comes thereafter is naught.

9] Rejoice, young man, in your youth, and let your heart cheer you in your youthful days. Follow

7] AND THE LIGHT IS SWEET ... The most pleasant things are here just for the taking. The light is sweet and it is a delight to see the sun illuminate the world in all its glory.

8] FOR IF A MAN LIVE MANY YEARS ... Life itself is a gift of Elohim, and if a man is privileged to live many years, why should he not free himself from slavery to material things so that he can really enjoy life?

REMEMBER . . .THE DAYS OF DARKNESS . . . Remember that this world is not all light and that every person is going to have days of darkness. Why add to the darkness? Every person will suffer frustrations and evil. Why add to your suffering? By becoming a slave to material things, by pursuing wealth endlessly, you only foster greed and discontent; you add to the darkness.

ALL THAT COMES THEREAFTER IS NAUGHT. After your lifetime there is no more opportunity to enjoy material pleasures. There is not even opportunity to perform good deeds. The hereafter is only a spiritual world of reward.

9] REJOICE ... LET YOUR HEART CHEER YOU ... A glad

בְּדַרְכֵי לִבְּךָ ובמראי [וּבְמַרְאֵה] עֵינֶיךָ וְדָע כִּי עַל־כָּל־
אֵלֶּה יְבִיאֲךָ הָאֱלֹהִים בַּמִּשְׁפָּט:
י וְהָסֵר כַּעַס מִלִּבֶּךָ וְהַעֲבֵר רָעָה מִבְּשָׂרֶךָ כִּי־הַיַּלְדוּת
וְהַשַּׁחֲרוּת הָבֶל:

והלך בדרכי לבך ובטוב תהיה, כי על־כל־אלה יביאך השופט במשפט: (י) והסר כעס. דברים המכעיסים את המקום: **והעבר רעה** — יצר הרע **מבשרך.** שיהיה לך לב בשר: **והשחרות.** נערות, שראש אדם שחור בימי עלומיו:

heart brings joy to the whole person; it refreshes body and mind.

FOLLOW THE DICTATES OF . . . HEART AND THE DESIRES OF . . . EYES . . . Most of man's thoughts and actions follow what the eye sees and reports to the heart. However, the dictates of the heart and the desires of the eyes are not always in the best interests of man in his relation to his fellow-man or in his relation to Elohim. Therefore . . .

KNOW THAT ELOHIM WILL BRING YOU TO JUDGMENT . . . Temper the passions of the heart and curb the desires of the eyes so that the resultant action will find favor in the eyes of man and Elohim. Your enjoyments should be such as will bring cheer in their aftermath as well as in the present.

10] REMOVE ANGER FROM YOUR HEART AND BANISH EVIL FROM YOUR BODY. Anger in the heart brings evil to the body

the dictates of your heart and the desires of your eyes, but know that Elohim will bring you to judgment for all these things.

10] Remove anger from your heart and banish evil from your body, for childhood and youth are fleeting.

in its wake. Here Koheleth reveals what has become common knowledge in recent times, that control of the emotions is the secret to cheerful and happy living. Tension developed in anger can produce depression and concomitant organic defects. This psychosomatic relationship must be taken into account if one seeks happiness. Greed and selfishness can bring on anger. Anger creates tension. Tension produces a high emotional state accompanied by powerful chemical changes in the body. Prolonged states of tension bring prolonged states of unhappiness, which in turn have deleterious effects on body and mind.

CHILDHOOD AND YOUTH . . . The years of creativity and productivity are not too many and, therefore, should be free from tension and anxiety.

ARE FLEETING. Here Koheleth gives the Hebrew word *hevel* its literal meaning: short and limited in duration, like a fleeting breath.

Chapter 12

MAN

What is man-degenerate
that you should remember him
and the son of mankind
that you should be mindful of him?
And yet you have made him
just a little less than Divine
and you have crowned him
with honor and dignity.

Psalms

א] וּזְכֹר אֶת־בּוֹרְאֶיךָ בִּימֵי בְּחוּרֹתֶיךָ עַד אֲשֶׁר לֹא־יָבֹאוּ יְמֵי
הָרָעָה וְהִגִּיעוּ שָׁנִים אֲשֶׁר תֹּאמַר אֵין־לִי בָהֶם חֵפֶץ׃

(א) **וזכר את־בוראך.** תמן תנינן (אבות פ״ג מ״א) עקביא בן מהללאל אומר הסתכל בשלשה דברים וכולי; וממקרא זה דרש (ירושלמי סוטה פ״ב ה״ב; ויקרא רבה פי״ח א) וזכור את בוראך — שתתן דין וחשבון לפניו; וזכור את בורך — קברך, מקום עפר רמה ותולעה; וזכור בארך — באר שנבעת ממקורה, היא טפה סרוחה של זרע ושל לובן: **ימי הרעה.** ימי הזקנה והחלשות (שבת קנא ע״ב; ויק״ר שם):

1 / The years of challenge

1] Remember . . . in the days of your youth . . . Koheleth continues in the vein of 11:9 and says, "Rejoice . . . but know." Paradoxically man is called upon to remember his responsibility to his Creator during the very years when he is told to rejoice. But this is, in essence, the message of all of Koheleth.

Elohim wants man to rejoice, to be happy and to enjoy a beautiful world. And yet man's joys must be guided by His commandments. This is not to diminish the joy but rather

1] Remember your Creator in the days of your youth, before the evil days come and the years draw near of which you will say, "I have no desire in them";

to steer man's joys into channels that will produce the optimum happiness for both body and spirit. The ability of man to control his emotions and to direct them into a course that will bring durable joy, and at the same time elevate him spiritually, is what distinguishes man from the lower animal.

The time for man to show that he can rise above the animal is in his youthful years. When man is challenged by worldly passions and desires and yet does not submit to the pleasures of the moment, then he shows his superiority. This is the trial that Elohim places before him.

BEFORE THE EVIL DAYS COME . . . Before the years of decline arrive, when man has lost most of his passion and desire. It does not take much courage to obey His commandments when one no longer has the desire for sin because of old age or feebleness.

ב) עַד אֲשֶׁר לֹא־תֶחְשַׁךְ הַשֶּׁמֶשׁ וְהָאוֹר וְהַיָּרֵחַ וְהַכּוֹכָבִים וְשָׁבוּ
הֶעָבִים אַחַר הַגָּשֶׁם׃
ג) בַּיּוֹם שֶׁיָּזֻעוּ שֹׁמְרֵי הַבַּיִת וְהִתְעַוְּתוּ אַנְשֵׁי הֶחָיִל וּבָטְלוּ
הַטֹּחֲנוֹת כִּי מִעֵטוּ וְחָשְׁכוּ הָרֹאוֹת בָּאֲרֻבּוֹת׃
ד) וְסֻגְּרוּ דְלָתַיִם בַּשּׁוּק בִּשְׁפַל קוֹל הַטַּחֲנָה וְיָקוּם לְקוֹל
הַצִּפּוֹר וְיִשַּׁחוּ כָּל־בְּנוֹת הַשִּׁיר׃

(ב) **עד אשר לא־תחשך השמש.** אמרו רבותינו (שבת קנא ע״ב, קנב ע״א; וע׳ קה״ר, ויק״ר שם) זו פדחת, שהיא מאירה ומצהבת באדם בחור, וכשמזקנת — היא מעלת קמטין ואין מצהבת; **והאור.** זה החוטם, שהוא תואר קלסתר פנים; **והירח.** זו נשמה שמאירה לאדם, שכיון שניטלה הימנו — אין לו מאור העיניים; **והכוכבים.** אלו הלסתות — רומני דאפי (עבודה זרה ל ע״ב) שקורין פומייל״ש (**pomejjals**, cheekbones) (של) [שהן] לחיים שמצהיבים: **ושבו העבים אחר הגשם.** תבוא כהיית המאור אחר דמעת הבכי מכמה צרות שעברו עליו: (ג) **שיזעו** — ירתיחו **שמרי הבית.** אלו הצלעות והכסלים המגינים על כל חלל הגוף; **והתעותו** — יאחלם עוות, שקורין קרנפ״א (**krampe**, cramps), והתעוותו — אנקרנפי״רונט בלעז (**inkrampiront**, be doubled up) **אנשי החיל.** אלו השוקיים שנשען כל הגוף עליהם: **ובטלו הטחנות.** אלו השיניים, **כי מעטו.** לעת זקנה רוב שיניו נושרות: **הראות בארבות.** אלו העיניים: (ד) **וסגרו דלתים.** אלו נקביו, **בשפל קול הטחנה.** קול ריחיים הטוחנים מאכל שבמעיו, והוא הקורקבן והמסס: **ויקום לקול הצפור.** שאפילו קול צפור מנערתו משנתו, משהזקין: **וישחו כל־בנות השיר.** כל קולות של כלי השיר דומות עליו (כשיחה) [כשוחה]; ולפי פשוטו משמעו — ישחו כמו ישפלו, כל שרים ושרות יהיו שפלים בעיניו, וכן ברזילי הגלעדי אמר לדוד (שמואל ב׳ יט: לו) אם־אשמע עוד

2–7 / The years of decline

2] BEFORE THE SUN, THE LIGHT ... ARE DARKENED ... In verses 2–7 Koheleth gives us a figurative and graphic description of man's last years. This famous passage should serve to remind man forcefully to utilize his formative years to greatest advantage. Before the lights are darkened — before creeping weakness and sickness, characteristic of the deterioration of the body, show their symptoms — that is the time to enjoy life.

2] before the sun, the light, the moon and the stars are darkened and the clouds return after the rain;

3] in the days when the keepers of the house shall tremble, and the strong men shall be bent, and the grinders cease because they are few, and those that stare through the windows will be darkened;

4] and the doors to the street will be shut and the voice of the mill will become low; when one will start at the sound of a bird and sounds of song will be muffled;

AND THE CLOUDS RETURN AFTER THE RAIN. Instead of clearing after the rain, the clouds return. Koheleth refers here to the chronic pains of old age, which may be relieved for the moment but always manage to return.

3] WHEN THE KEEPERS OF THE HOUSE SHALL TREMBLE . . . According to the Rabbis, when the ribs, the skeletal structure which protects the inner vital organs, begin to weaken and tremble.

THE STRONG MEN SHALL BE BENT . . . The knees begin to shake.

THE GRINDERS CEASE . . . The teeth cease to function properly because they are too few.

THOSE THAT STARE THROUGH THE WINDOWS . . . The eyes that look out through their sockets.

4] THE DOORS TO THE STREET ARE SHUT . . . The apertures and organs of excretion cease to function properly.

ה) גַּם מִגָּבֹהַּ יִרָאוּ וְחַתְחַתִּים בַּדֶּרֶךְ וְיָנֵאץ הַשָּׁקֵד וְיִסְתַּבֵּל
הֶחָגָב וְתָפֵר הָאֲבִיּוֹנָה כִּי־הֹלֵךְ הָאָדָם אֶל־בֵּית עוֹלָמוֹ
וְסָבְבוּ בַשּׁוּק הַסֹּפְדִים:

ו) עַד אֲשֶׁר לֹא־ירחק [יֵרָתֵק] חֶבֶל הַכֶּסֶף וְתָרֻץ גֻּלַּת הַזָּהָב
וְתִשָּׁבֶר כַּד עַל־הַמַּבּוּעַ וְנָרֹץ הַגַּלְגַּל אֶל־הַבּוֹר:

בקול שרים ושרות: (ה) **גם מגבה יראו** מגבשושיות ותלוליות שברחובות, הוא דואג לצאת לשוק פן יכשל בהם; **וחתחתים בדרך.** אימות וחתות הרבה בדרכים יש לו. חתחתים — לשון כפול בתיבה, כמו גלגלים, קשקשים, זלזלים: **וינאץ.** לשון (שה״ש ז:יג) הנצו הרמונים, שהרי האל״ף לא נקראת בה; [השקד]. אמרו רבותינו, זו קליבוסת, הנק״א בלעז (**hanke**, haunch, hip), שעצם הירך תקוע בה, ובזקנותו בשרו כחוש והעצם בולט כמו נץ האילן שהוא בולט; וינאץ השקד — אילן של שקדים; כלומר, שתקפוץ הזקנה עליו כשקד זה הממהר להנץ לפני כל האילנות: **ויסתבל החגב.** אלו העגבות, שיהיו עגבותיו דומות עליו כסובל משא כבד. ויסתבל — אידאייר״ט שורפישיי״ץ בלעז (*éd ért sorféséiz,* and will be overburdened); **ותפר האביונה.** חמדת תאות נשים, שאינו נזקק לנשים לתשמיש. אביונה — תאוה, כמו (דברים א:כו) ולא אביתם, (תהלים קיט:קעד) תאבתי לישועתך: (ו) **עד אשר לא־ירתק חבל הכסף.** זה חוט השדרה, שהוא לבן ככסף, ובמותו חסר מוחו ומתרוקן ויבש ומתעקם בתוך החליות ונעשה כשלשלת. ירתק — לשון (ישעיה מ:יט) ורתקות כסף: **ותרץ גלת הזהב.** זו האמה, שהיתה מקלחת מים ונובעת כמעיין, כמו (יהושע טו:יט) גלת עליות. ותרץ — לשון רציצה: **ותשבר כד על־המבוע.** זה הכרס, שהיא עבה ונבקעת במותו: **ונרץ הגלגל אל־הבור.** יתרוצץ גלגל העין בתוך גומא; ולפי פשוטו — גלגל הדולין בו מים מן הבור. כך נדרש כל העניין במסכת שבת (ע״ש): ומדרש קינות (איכה רבה פתיחתא כג; וע׳ קה״ר, קה״ז) פותרו כנגד כל ישראל; (א־ז) **וזכר את־בוראך בימי בחורתיך** — בעוד שהבחורות שבכם קיימות; בעוד שהכהונה קיימת, שנאמר בה (שמואל א׳ ב:כח) ובחר אתו מכל־שבטי ישראל לי לכהן; בעוד שהלוייה קיימת, שנאמר בה (דברים יח:ה) כי בו בחר ה׳ אלהיך מכל־שבטיך; בעוד שמלכות בית דוד קיימת, שנאמר בה (תהלים עח:ע) ויבחר בדוד עבדו; בעוד שירושלם קיימת, שנאמר בה (מלכים א׳ יא:לב) העיר אשר בחרתי בה; בעוד שבית הבחירה

THE VOICE OF THE MILL WILL BECOME LOW . . . There is a slowdown in the working of the digestive organs which refine the coarse food.

5] when one will fear heights, and terrors will lurk on the way, and the almond will have blossomed; when one will appear stooped like an overloaded grasshopper, and the desire will fail — because man is going to his eternal rest, and therefore the mourners walk about in the street;

6] before the silver cord is snapped and the golden bowl is shattered, and the pitcher is broken at the fountain, and the wheel falls shattered into the pit.

START AT THE SOUND OF A BIRD . . . When sleep is restless and even the sound of a bird is sufficient to awaken one.

AND THE SOUNDS OF SONG WILL BE MUFFLED. The senses are impaired and the sound of song is no longer appreciated.

5] WHEN ONE WILL FEAR HEIGHTS . . . To the old man even a small incline appears to be a high mountain.

AND TERRORS LURK ON THE WAY . . . Even insignificant obstacles become great annoyances.

AND THE ALMOND WILL HAVE BLOSSOMED . . . The almond is one of the fastest and earliest-growing trees. The allusion here is to the fast-growing boils and tumors of old age.

STOOPED LIKE AN OVERLOADED GRASSHOPPER . . . The aged man is often stooped and bent close to the ground as though he were carrying a heavy load.

MOURNERS WALK ABOUT . . . anticipating death and preparing the last rites.

6] BEFORE THE SILVER CORD IS SNAPPED . . . Because of their vital functions, the spinal cord is referred to as the silver

ז) וְיָשֹׁב הֶעָפָר עַל־הָאָרֶץ כְּשֶׁהָיָה וְהָרוּחַ תָּשׁוּב אֶל־הָאֱלֹהִים
אֲשֶׁר נְתָנָהּ:

קיימת, שנאמר בו (דברי הימים ב׳ ז:טז) ועתה בחרתי והקדשתי [את] הבית הזה; בעוד שאתם קיימים, שנאמר (דברים ז:ו) בך בחר ה׳ [אלהיך]; **עד אשר לא־יבאו ימי הרעה.** אלו ימי הגולה: **עד אשר לא־תחשך השמש.** זו מלכות בית דוד, שנאמר (תהלים פט:לז) וכסאו כשמש נגדי; **והאור.** זו תורה, שנאמר (משלי ו:כג) כי נר מצוה ותורה אור; **והירח.** זו סנהדרין, דתנן (סנהדרין פ״ד מ״ג) סנהדרין היתה כחצי גורן עגולה; **והכוכבים.** אלו הרבנים, שנאמר (דניאל יב:ג) ומצדיקי הרבים ככוכבים: **ושבו העבים אחר הגשם** — צרה אחר צרה קשה; אתה מוצא בכל הנבואות הקשות שנתנבא עליהם ירמיהו, לא באו עליהם אלא לאחר חורבן הבית: **ביום שיזעו שמרי הבית.** אלו משמרות כהונה ולויה: **והתעותו אנשי החיל.** אלו הכהנים, שהם גבורים בכח: אמר ר׳ אבא בר כהנא, עשרים ושנים אלף לויים הניף אהרן ביום אחד; אמר ר׳ חנינא, המוראה הזו דבר קל הוא והכהן זורקה יותר משלשים אמה (זבחים סד ע״א): **ובטלו הטחנות.** אלו המשניות הגדולות, משנת ר׳ עקיבא ומשנת ר׳ חייא ומשנת בר קפרא: **וחשכו הראות.** שישתכח התלמוד מן הלב: **וסגרו דלתים בשוק.** כגון דלתי נחושתא (בר) [בת] אלנתן שהיו פתוחין לרווחה, **בשפל קול הטחנה** — על ידי שלא נתעסקו בתורה; אמר ר׳ שמואל, נמשלו ישראל לטחינת הריחיים, מה ריחיים אינן בטילות לא ביום ולא בלילה, אף כאן (יהושע א:ח) והגית בו יומם ולילה: **ויקום לקול הצפור.** זה נבוכדנצר הרשע; אמר ר׳ לוי (ע׳ מדרש תהלים עט:א) שמונה עשרה שנה היתה בת קול יוצאה ומפוצצת בפלטין נבוכדנצר עבדא בישא זיל אחריב ביתיה דמרך דבני מרך לא שמעין ליה; **וישחו כל־בנות השיר.** [שעלה וביטל השיר מבית המשתה, דכתיב] (ישעיה כד:ט) בשיר לא ישתו־יין: **גם מגבה ייראו.** מגבוהו של עולם יתיירא וידאג לבו, פן יעשה בו כאשר עשה בראשונים; **וחתחתים בדרך.** מתוך כך יבקש לו אותות ורמזים אם יצליח בדרך שילך, כעניין שנאמר (יחזקאל כא:כו) כי־עמד מלך־בבל (על) [אל]־אם הדרך [וגו׳] לקסם־קסם קלקל בחצים שאל בתרפים: **וינאץ השקד.** תצמח נבואת ירמיה, שנאמר (ירמיה א:יא) מקל שקד אני ראה; אמר ר׳ אלעזר (ע׳ ירושלמי תענית פ״ד ה״ה) השקד הזה, משעה שהוא מציץ [מניץ — מוציא את נצו] עד שהוא גומר פירותיו עשרים ואחד יום, כך משבעה עשר בתמוז עד תשעה באב עשרים ואחד יום: **ויסתבל החגב.** זה צלמו של נבוכדנצר — (דניאל ג:א) רומה אמין שתין פתיה אמין שת, ואם אין בעוביו שליש [אלא שש, רש״י שם] אינו יכול לעמוד, ואת אמרת (שם) אקימה בבקעת דורא? אמר רב ביבי, מעמידין אותו ונופל, מעמידין אותו ונופל, עד שהביאו כל זהב שבירושלם ושפכו דימוס על רגליו, לקיים מה שנאמר (יחזקאל ז:יט) וזהבם לנדה יהיה;

7] And the dust returns to the earth as it was originally, and the spirit returns to Elohim who gave it.

ותפר האביונה. זו זכות אבות — תופר משענת אבות שלכם; ויהיה אביונה מלשון אב: **כי־הלך האדם.** ישראל שנקראו (צאן) [אדם, שנאמר] (יחזקאל לד: לא) אדם אתם (יבמות סא ע״א), **אל־בית עלמו.** מבבל באו, לבבל חזרו — תרח אבי אברהם מעבר הנהר היה; **וסבבו שוק הסופדים.** גלות יכניה קדמה לגלות צדקיה אחת עשרה שנה; כשהגלה נבוכדנצר את גלות צדקיה בקולרין, היו יוצאין גלות יכניה לקראת נבוכדנצר על כרחן עם שאר בני העיר לקלסו שהוא גבור ומצליח, והיו רואין את השבויים ושואלין אותם איש על קרובו מה נעשה בו, והיו משיבין אותן (ירמיה טו: ב) אשר למות למות (ואשר לשבי לשבי) ואשר לחרב לחרב, והיו מקלסין בידם אחת ובידם אחרת מספקין ומטפחין הספד על אחיהם ועל בניהם: **עד אשר לא־ירתק חבל הכסף.** זו שלשלת יוחסין; **ותרץ גלת הזהב.** אלו דברי תורה, שנאמר (תהלים יט: יא) הנחמדים מזהב; **ותשבר כד על־המבוע.** כדו של ברוך בן נריה על מבועו של ירמיהו, ששניהם גלו לבבל ופסקו מלימודם בעוני הדרך; תחילה גלו למצרים שהגלם יוחנן בן קרח, וכשהחריב נבוכדנצר את מצרים הגלם לבבל; **ונרץ הגלגל אל־הבור.** זו בבל, שהיא זוטו של עולם: **וישב העפר וגומר.** מבבל באו, לבבל חזרו; **והרוח תשוב.** זו רוח הקדש, שכיון שנסתלקה רוח הקדש — גלו:

cord and the brain as the golden bowl. When the spinal cord is severed then nervous communication is destroyed and deterioration of brain and body follow.

THE PITCHER IS BROKEN . . . When the rope snaps at a well, the wheel at one end and the pitcher at the other are both shattered.

7] THE DUST RETURNS . . . The body disintegrates to become part of the soil. "Dust thou art and to dust thou returneth" (Gen. 3:19).

ח] הֲבֵל הֲבָלִים אָמַר הַקּוֹהֶלֶת הַכֹּל הָבֶל׃
ט] וְיֹתֵר שֶׁהָיָה קֹהֶלֶת חָכָם עוֹד לִמַּד־דַּעַת אֶת־הָעָם וְאִזֵּן
וְחִקֵּר תִּקֵּן מְשָׁלִים הַרְבֵּה׃

(ח) **הבל הבלים** אני רואה בעולם **אמר הקוהלת.** מי שבו קבוצת החכמה: **הבל הבלים** — כל מה שנברא בששת ימי בראשית: (ט) **ויתר שהיה קהלת חכם.** ויותר ממה שנכתב בספר זה, היה קהלת חכם: **ואזן.** עשה אזנים לתורה, כקופה זו שאין לה אזנים לאחוז בה ובא [שלמה] ועשה להם אזנים, שתיקן עירובין לסייג לשמירת שבת, ותיקן נטילת ידים סייג לטהרה, וגזר על השניות סייג

8–14 / Summary

8] VANITY OF VANITIES . . . ALL IS VANITY. Dramatically, Koheleth returns to his opening verse (1:2) as if to say: let us re-evaluate this verse that has become the maxim of *kahal* and the axiom of the materialists.

There are vanities in the universe, true, but they should not be interpreted to signify that life is empty of value. On the contrary, life should be viewed from the many good aspects of the universe and from the many blessings of man.

The vanities must be seen as those ways of Elohim that the human mind cannot grasp. In spite of these seeming imperfections, man can find happiness. In fact, the greatest happiness is attained when man views the imperfections as challenges to be overcome.

There are anomalies; there are righteous people who suffer and wicked people who prosper.

There are inequities: there are fools who end up in better positions than the wise.

8] Vanity of vanities, says Koheleth, all is vanity.
9] Aside from being wise, Koheleth taught the people knowledge, he weighed and probed and fashioned many proverbs.

There is evil: there are people who slave for wealth all their lives and then lose that wealth.

In spite of all these vanities, you are expected to be grateful for the many good things: life itself, sun, food, health, family, the beautiful and the harmonious. You are expected to enjoy life, to be content with what you have, to perform good deeds, to fear Elohim, and to follow in His commandments.

"All is vanity." As far as the human mind is concerned, the universe is an imperfect one and it is futile for man to try to understand evil. Nevertheless, if one will appreciate all that is good in the universe, life can be beautiful.

9] ASIDE FROM BEING WISE ... The Bible (I Kings 5:11) describes him as the "wisest of men."

KOHELETH TAUGHT, WEIGHED AND PROBED ... The thinking of Koheleth was further refined and clarified because he taught his wisdom to the people. The great teacher must digest, organize and verify his subject matter before presenting it to his audience. Teaching and carrying on discussions with the people make for the greater accuracy and validity of one's conclusions.

AND FASHIONED MANY PROVERBS. To further refine his thinking and to make it palatable to his audience, Koheleth presented it in the form of proverbs.

י] בִּקֵּשׁ קֹהֶלֶת לִמְצֹא דִּבְרֵי־חֵפֶץ וְכָתוּב יֹשֶׁר דִּבְרֵי אֱמֶת׃

יא] דִּבְרֵי חֲכָמִים כַּדָּרְבֹנוֹת וּכְמַשְׂמְרוֹת נְטוּעִים בַּעֲלֵי אֲסֻפּוֹת
נִתְּנוּ מֵרֹעֶה אֶחָד׃

יב] וְיֹתֵר מֵהֵמָּה בְּנִי הִזָּהֵר עֲשׂוֹת סְפָרִים הַרְבֵּה אֵין קֵץ וְלַהַג
הַרְבֵּה יְגִעַת בָּשָׂר׃

לעריות (עירובין כא ע״ב, יבמות כא ע״א; וע׳ רש״י שם): **(י) בקש קהלת.** נתן לבו וחזר על הדבר ומצאו: **דברי חפץ.** הלכה למשה מסיני: **וכתוב ישר.** זה תורה שבכתב והנביאים: **(יא) דברי חכמים** שעשו סייג לתורה בגזירות להרחיק את האדם מן העבירה, כגון אכילת קדשים עד השחר והם אמרו עד חצות, וקריאת שמע דערבית כמו כן, **כדרבנות.** מה דרבן זה מכוון את הפרה לתלמיה — כך דבריהם מכוונים את האדם לדרכי חיים, **וכמשמרות נטועים.** מה מסמר זה קבוע — אף דבריהם קבועים, ומה נטיעה פרה ורבה — אף דבריהם פרים ורבים למצוא בהם טעם: **בעלי אספות.** מסמרים שיש להם גולגולת אסופה וגסה, גרו״ס בלעז (grose, large) — כן פירשו דונש בן לברט: **נתנו מרעה אחד.** כל דבריהם דברי אלהים חיים (ע׳ עירובין יג ע״ב), הוא אמרן, ורועה אחד נתנן — משה מפי הגבורה (חגיגה ג ע״ב; תנחומא וילך א): **וכמשמרות.** כתוב בשי״ן, שהתורה בעשרים וארבעה ספרים וכמנין משמרות כהונה ולויה (ירושלמי שבת פ״ו ה״ב; תנחומא שם): **(יב) ויתר מהמה בני הזהר.** ויותר מיושר דברי אמת, דברים הכתובים בספרים הנזכרים למעלה, **בני הזהר** לשמור דברי חכמים; ואם תאמר, אם יש בהם צורך, למה לא נכתבו? **עשות ספרים הרבה אין קץ.** אם באנו לכתוב, לא הספקנו, **ולהג הרבה יגעת**

10] SOUGHT TO DISCOVER DESIRABLE KNOWLEDGE . . . Koheleth sought explanation of the ways of Elohim in the universe; he sought to understand the basis for good and evil.

THAT WHICH WAS WRITTEN . . . Koheleth read all the books that were written by the wise men of all nations in their attempts to advise on correct living and in their attempts to explain the true meaning of natural phenomena.

11] THE WORDS OF THE WISE SERVE AS GOADS . . . Just as the goad, a pointed rod, directs the animal along the right path, so the words of the wise are the best guides for the human. Koheleth stresses that in matters of the spirit and

10] Koheleth sought to discover desirable knowledge; he perused that which was written on correct living and on the true meaning of things.

11] The words of the wise serve as goads; they are like well-fastened nails with broad heads; all were given by one Shepherd.

12] Beyond the guidance of the wise, my son, exercise caution; of buying and writing books there is no end, and much study will only wear your strength away.

knowledge of Elohim, the best sources are the wise. They have always pondered these matters; they are therefore the best guides. Only in consultation with the wise can one develop a world-view that encompasses all of life.

WELL-FASTENED NAILS WITH BROAD HEADS . . . The words of the wise are the result of much probing and experience and are therefore well-founded and durable. And the words of the wise (the well-fastened nails) have broad heads. They can be removed, re-examined and restudied to see what the wise have to say for the changing times and changing generations: the words of the wise are profound, and one can always benefit by studying and restudying them.

ALL WERE GIVEN BY ONE SHEPHERD. Do not expect that you will be able to learn more about Elohim than has already been uncovered by the wise. For all the thoughts and all the heights attained by the wise were granted them by the one Shepherd, and He has allowed them as much as the limited human mind is able to conceive.

12] BEYOND THE GUIDANCE OF THE WISE . . . Koheleth warns against attempts to supersede the wise. Books and much study

יג] סוֹף דָּבָר הַכֹּל נִשְׁמָע אֶת־הָאֱלֹהִים יְרָא וְאֶת־מִצְוֺתָיו
שְׁמוֹר כִּי־זֶה כָּל־הָאָדָם׃
יד] כִּי אֶת־כָּל־מַעֲשֶׂה הָאֱלֹהִים יָבִא בְמִשְׁפָּט עַל כָּל־נֶעְלָם
אִם־טוֹב וְאִם־רָע׃

סוֹף דָּבָר הַכֹּל נִשְׁמָע אֶת־הָאֱלֹהִים יְרָא וְאֶת־מִצְוֺתָיו שְׁמוֹר כִּי־זֶה כָּל־הָאָדָם׃

בשר. ואם לתת לב לגירסא חבילות יותר ממה שאין הלב משיג, יגיעה היא לבריות שאין להשיג; ואל יאמר, הואיל ולא אוכל לגמור המלאכה למה אתחיל? אך (יג) **סוף דבר הכל נשמע את־האלהים ירא.** מה שתוכל — עשה ולבך לשמים, **ואת־מצותיו שמור כי־זה כל־האדם.** כי לדבר הזה נברא כל האדם: (יד) **כי את־כל־מעשה** אשר אדם עושה **יבא האלהים במשפט**; ולכך נקוד מעשה פתח והטעם למעלה, לפי שאינו דבוק לשם: **על כל־נעלם** — אפילו על השוגג, **אם־טוב ואם־רע** — אפילו נכשל במצות, כגון נותן צדקה לעני בפרהסיא:
סוף דבר הכל נשמע את־האלהים ירא ואת־מצותיו שמור כי־זה כל־האדם:

in this area will only wear away a person's strength in endless search for what is beyond the human mind.

Koheleth has already informed us (8:17) that it is impossible for man to understand the supermundane ways of Elohim.

13] In sum . . . After all the discussion in regard to life and its meaning; in regard to the search for happiness; in regard of the fulfillment of man's purpose . . .

fear Elohim and keep His commandments . . . Man is basically an animal. Potentially, he can control his animal instincts. But if undisciplined, he becomes a slave to passion and a purveyor of greed, jealousy, deception and tyranny. No man-made law can effectively make man master of his animal tendencies in public and in private. Only as man recognizes Elohim in the universe and subjects himself to His discipline (fear of Elohim) will he be able to rise above the level of the animal.

Only as man keeps His commandments will he feel His

13] In sum, after all has been heard, fear Elohim and keep His commandments; for that is all of man.
14] For Elohim will bring every deed to judgment, even every hidden motive, for good or for evil.

Omnipresence and thus control his emotions, passions and greed. When man has gained this control he is above the animal and he is able to command respect and to honor the dignity of his fellow-man.

THAT IS ALL OF MAN. The ability to subject himself to the guidance of Elohim, the ability to control his emotions and passions — that is what distinguishes man from the animal.

14] FOR ELOHIM WILL BRING EVERY DEED ... For man to elevate himself above the animal level, he must believe that there is an Elohim and that there must be a hereafter. For only then can he believe that he is accountable for his deeds and way of living.

Every deed will be brought before the bar of judgment for evaluation before reward or punishment is meted out.

EVEN EVERY HIDDEN MOTIVE ... Not only is there a quantitative reckoning of the number of good or evil deeds, but there is, also, a qualitative judgment of each individual deed. Was the motive of the good deed genuine and pure? Was the evil deed premeditated or unintentional? All nuances and impulses as well as consequences are considered by Elohim at the bar of justice.

The human mind, due to its limitations, cannot account for all that occurs in the universe. Despite these limitations, the presence of Elohim in the universe can be felt by all. If man will attach himself to Elohim and guide himself by His Commandments, he can rise above the animal and attain the maximum of happiness allotted to him — as man.

ת ו נ ש ל ב ע